The Arms Trade and Europe

CHATHAM HOUSE PAPERS

An International Security Programme Publication
Programme Director: Professor Sir Laurence Martin

The Royal Institute of International Affairs, at Chatham House in London, has provided an impartial forum for discussion and debate on current international issues for 75 years. Its resident research fellows, specialized information resources, and range of publications, conferences, and meetings span the fields of international politics, economics, and security. The Institute is independent of government.

CHATHAM HOUSE PAPERS

The Arms Trade and Europe

Paul Cornish

THE ROYAL INSTITUTE
OF INTERNATIONAL
AFFAIRS

Pinter
A Cassell Imprint
Wellington House, 125 Strand, London WC2R 0BB, United Kingdom

First published in 1995

British Library Cataloguing in Publication Data
A CIP catalogue record for this book is available from the British Library

ISBN 1-85567-285-5 (Paperback)
      1-85567-284-7 (Hardback)

Typeset by Koinonia Limited
Printed and bound in Great Britain by
Biddles Limited, Guildford and King's Lynn

Contents

Acknowledgments

I am grateful to colleagues at Chatham House for their guidance and help in the course of my research, in particular Professor Sir Laurence Martin, Professor Jack Spence and Professor Trevor Taylor. The Chatham House study group which followed this project from its inception was a vital source of criticism, ideas and information. I am grateful to all who attended the meetings, or who provided comments in writing, for giving so generously of their time and energy. I should also like to thank those politicians and officials in Britain, Europe and the Far East who agreed to be interviewed. My participation in the Cameron Commission of Inquiry in Cape Town in June 1995 was an unexpected opportunity to review some of the issues which I address here, in a particularly open and refreshing environment, and I am grateful to the Commissioners and their staff. My collaborator in this project has been Dr Joachim Krause of the Deutsche Gesellschaft für Auswärtige Politik in Bonn, and I am grateful to him and the DGAP for their congenial and constructive approach to the project. Without the efforts of Dr Peter van Ham and the Western European Union Institute for Security Studies, the conference which was held in Paris towards the end of this project would not have been the success it was. In Chatham House, Margaret May, Emma Matanle, Hannah Doe, Tom Lee and the staff of the library have all helped in the production and publication of this paper. Lastly, special thanks are due to the Volkswagen Stiftung for so generously supporting this project.

Plenty of thanks, but no blame; any errors of fact, logic or judgment are, of course, entirely my own.

September 1995   Paul Cornish

Abbreviations and acronyms

ACA	Agency for the Control of Armaments (WEU)
ACDA	Arms Control and Disarmament Agency (US)
AG	Australia Group
CAT	Conventional Arms Transfer
CBW	chemical, biological weapons
CCP	Common Commercial Policy (EC)
CFSP	Common Foreign and Security Policy
CoCom	Coordinating Committee for Multilateral Export Controls
CRL	Common Reference List
CSCE	Conference on Security and Cooperation in Europe
EC/U	European Community/Union
EDEM	European Defence Equipment Market
EEC	European Economic Community
EP	European Parliament
EPC	European Political Cooperation
EPCI	Enhanced Proliferation Control Initiative
FCO	Foreign and Commonwealth Office (UK)
GATT	General Agreement on Tariffs and Trade
GPS	global positioning satellite
IAEL	International Atomic Energy List (CoCom)
IEPG	Independent European Programme Group
IGC(PU)	Intergovernmental Conference (Political Union)
IIL	International Industrial List (CoCom)
IML	International Munitions List (CoCom)
MAP	Military Assistance Program
MBT	main battle tank
MTCR	Missile Technology Control Regime

NATO	North Atlantic Treaty Organization
NBC	nuclear, biological, chemical
NSG	Nuclear Suppliers Group
QMV	qualified majority voting
SEA	Single European Act
SEM	Single European Market
SIPRI	Stockholm International Peace Research Institute
TEU	Treaty on European Union ('Maastricht Treaty')
WEAG	Western European Armaments Group
WEU	Western European Union
WMD	weapons of mass destruction

For me there is only one true morality; but it might not fit you, as you do not manufacture aerial battleships. There is only one true morality for every man; but every man has not the same true morality.

ANDREW UNDERSHAFT, ARMS MANUFACTURER, IN ACT I OF G.B. SHAW'S *MAJOR BARBARA* (1906)

A Westerner who wants to grapple with this subject must try, for a few minutes, to slip out of his native Western skin and look at the encounter between the world and the West through the eyes of the great non-Western majority of mankind.

ARNOLD TOYNBEE, DIRECTOR OF STUDIES, CHATHAM HOUSE, BBC REITH LEC-TURES (1952)

If you have scruples, don't sell arms at all.

MAHATHIR MOHAMAD, PRIME MINISTER OF MALAYSIA (MARCH 1995)

Chapter 1

Introduction

This study addresses recent efforts by the member states of the European Union (EU) to devise common procedures by which to supervise and regulate their involvement in the international trade in weapons and related technology. The study is concerned with the trade in 'conventional' weapons and weapons platforms, such as armoured fighting vehicles, artillery, combat aircraft and warships, and associated technology. It does not examine the illegal or covert international trade in conventional and other weapons, nor does it address the proliferation of nuclear, biological and chemical weapons of mass destruction.

As the Cold War drew to a close from the mid-1980s, military spending around the world began to fall. Domestic arms markets contracted and the size of the global trade in weapons, military equipment and related technology began a steep decline. The international arms market not only shrank, but its character and dynamics also began to change dramatically. With mounting public pressure for a 'peace dividend', and the acceptance by governments that Cold War levels of military spending and deployment were no longer necessary or justifiable, the Cold War protagonists soon found themselves with large excesses in defence manufacturing capacity. Defence industries and governments identified a number of possible courses of action, including defence conversion, diversification out of defence manufacturing, industrial consolidation and restructuring within the defence sector, and weapons exports. Conversion of manufacturing plants from military to civilian production was widely discussed but was soon perceived to be something less than the cure-all for which many had hoped. In the West, the claims for defence conversion were met with a sceptical response, particularly from those governments which took a free-market approach

1

to defence industrial restructuring after the Cold War. In the former Soviet Union and among its allies, it was realized that the only marketable, hard-currency-earning commodity was weapons – good, relatively cheap swords, rather than badly marketed, over-engineered ploughshares. Diversification, whereby defence industries, conglomerates and multinationals expand and acquire non-military sectors, met with a more favourable response in industry, especially in the West. But diversification proved to be difficult, and many firms found that expertise and knowledge accumulated in the defence sector did not travel well. The third option was received rather more favourably. A great deal of effort has been devoted to national and international restructuring and consolidation in the defence sector, and some firms have even shaken off non-military interests altogether.

In spite of narrowing prospects for overseas sales, the export option was also seized upon by the defence industry. At a time of global recession, governments, too, were interested in a course which could enable 'vital' or 'strategic' national industries to be sustained, unit production costs to be reduced and further research and development to be funded. The scene was thus set for a 'new age of export driven proliferation'.[1] With similar conclusions being reached throughout the defence manufacturing world, it appeared that the 'peaceful' post-Cold War world would have an arms market which, although considerably smaller, would in many respects be more diverse, vigorous and competitive than its Cold War predecessor. With huge excesses in supply combined with declining demand, it would also be a market in which much of the initiative had shifted to the buyer. As this shift took place, so the struggle for market share became increasingly competitive. Defence export decisions became ever more responsive to commercial considerations and contracts became increasingly complex, often involving the transfer of manufacturing plants, 'knowhow' and key, sensitive technologies through offset and countertrade arrangements. The development of the buyer's market also inhibited efforts to control defence-related trade. At the national level, no matter how rigorous their export-control policies and practices, individual governments saw that the glut of old and new suppliers meant that any decision to deny a given export might simply result in the buyer going elsewhere; the complaint that 'if we don't export, others will' was heard increasingly. Competition for market share also diminished the chance for wider supply-side consensus on the control of exports of certain weapons or technologies to certain destinations, making multilateral supply-side regulation of the defence trade increasingly difficult.

The end of the Cold War not only saw the advantage, in market terms, passing to the buyer; it also saw the buyer becoming rather more self-assured. During the Cold War, non-aligned or Third World states felt themselves to be in a struggle to achieve the dignity and respect due to them as full members of the international system of states. Nowhere was the sense of dissatisfaction more plain than in the United Nations. As the membership of the UN expanded rapidly during the 1950s and 1960s, so discrepancies were perceived between the Charter's promises regarding the sovereign equality of states, and the *Realpolitik* of a world dominated by the superpower confrontation. But with the passing of the Cold War, the promises made in the UN Charter are now expected to be honoured. Aware of their increasing importance in the international economic system, Third World states have become far less willing to accept second-class status. For these states, the end of the Cold War is the triumph of nationhood and state sovereignty, and the end of the decades-long struggle for decolonization and full membership of the international system. Their sense of frustration has been apparent for many years, but what distinguishes the current mood is that many governments and leaders feel able to add substance to the rhetoric. Technological, economic and even military advantages are still enjoyed by the West/North, and there is no doubt that these advantages confer a certain authority and bargaining strength over Third World customers. But as these states assume an increasingly important role in the global economy, the West's potential for 'leverage' is likely to become more limited.

With manufacturers anxious to sell, particularly in the 'boom' market of the Asia-Pacific region, and with an increasingly assertive and self-confident clientele, the international trade in conventional weapons and related technology is changing in two important ways. First, with so much more now being heard of a state's right, under Article 51 of the UN Charter, to defend itself and, by extension, to decide for itself what, and from whom, to buy in the arms market, the manufacture of weapons and the trade in them are increasingly seen in national terms. The ownership of modern conventional weapons, and the ability to manufacture them, are now widely held to be normal, inalienable and even essential attributes of a modern, sovereign nation-state. The international arms trade is best described and understood in 'systemic' terms, as an elaborate network of relationships between various national interest groups on the one hand, and internationally between suppliers and recipients on the other.[2] But what is becoming clear is that the dynamic behind the modern arms trade – and the main obstacle to its regulation – is the new, self-confident nationalism of the post-Cold War era. The second important feature of the contemporary arms trade is the absence of an internationally accepted, central organizing principle. Many of the conditions which underpinned the hegemonic arms trade relationships of the Cold War have now been undermined. It is no longer possible to describe the international arms trade primarily as an extension of East–West power politics, or even as the manifestation of the foreign policy of the world's weapon manufacturers and suppliers. But if it is clear that the trade is no longer organized along the relatively simple lines of Cold War power politics, it is much less obvious what, if anything, could provide a new organizational core. The international arms market is more commercially oriented than at any time during the Cold War, but it seems unlikely that the market alone will be able to provide the political and moral principles and procedures by which the trade should, arguably, be regulated. With the 'new world order' offering very little in the way of controlling mechanisms, even at the most basic level of Cold-War-style spheres of influence, something approaching political and economic free trade in arms may have arrived.

In August 1990 Iraq invaded Kuwait and the ostensibly revitalized UN and the 'international community' faced their first major challenge. Following Iraq's defeat, information about the ease with which Saddam Hussein had played the international arms market, and the embarrassing provenance of much of Iraq's weaponry, suggested to many that an unregulated or poorly regulated international arms market was not acceptable. A rush of declarations and initiatives then followed: the declarations of June 1991 and January 1992 by the Conference on Security and Cooperation in Europe (CSCE) and the subsequent publication in November 1993 of 'Principles and Guidelines governing Conventional Arms Transfers'; the Group of Seven's 'Declaration on Conventional Arms Transfers and NBC Non-Proliferation' in July 1991; the 'Guidelines for Conventional Arms Transfers' issued by the Permanent Five members of the Security Council in October 1991; and the UN's Conventional Arms Register launched in December 1991. By mid-1995, however, none of these initiatives had achieved much of note, if achievement is measured in terms of restraining the eagerness with which established arms suppliers exploit the international export market.

The member states of the European Union occupy a very large share of the international arms market. In 1993, according to the US Arms Control and Disarmament Agency, the fifteen states that are now members of the EU together exported conventional weapons and military equipment worth US$6,950 million – some 32 per cent of the world total.[3] Using different counting methods, the US Congressional Research Service described France as the leading weapons supplier to the developing world in 1994.[4] The governments concerned, and the institutions of the EU, have sought to bring a degree of organization to these activities. The object of this book is to describe EU involvement in various aspects of the international arms trade, and to assess the potential for a common EU system or code by which to manage that involvement. Is there anything about the politics, organization and structure of the EU which suggests that this important group of supplier states will succeed where others have so far been unable or unwilling to practise self-restraint?

One signal lesson of the Iraqi arms build-up was that the transfer of weapon manufacturing technology, and dual-use technology, can over time prove to be as significant as transfers of completed weapons. The modern 'arms' trade has to be understood as involving weapons of varying sophistication, tangible technology of both military and civil origin, and intangible 'know-how'. Yet the peculiarities of EU treaty law, and the preferences and prejudices of several member governments, require distinctions to be drawn between the transfer of completed weapons and military equipment on one hand, and manufacturing technology on the other. Accordingly, Chapter 2 reviews west European involvement in the arms trade and its regulation since 1945, leaving the trade in certain types of technology to be discussed in Chapter 3. The scene having been set, the next three chapters make a more analytical contribution. Chapter 4 examines the commercial and industrial obstacles to effective EU regulation. Turning to the politics of European integration, Chapter 5 assesses the scope for cooperation in foreign, security and defence policies in the EU, and gauges the likely effect on multilateral export regulation. Chapter 6 completes the discussion by looking outside the confines of the EU at the conceptual side of arms-trade regulation, and particularly at the problem of defining and sustaining a central, universal code of practice. Chapter 7 summarizes the discussion and offers some concluding comments.

Chapter 2
Weapons

Introduction

There could be no better site than western Europe for a laboratory dedicated to the research of the modern (post-1945) arms trade. Here, most aspects and functions of the arms trade have been experienced and discussed: import; research and development; sole, collaborative and licensed manufacture; export; and unilateral and multilateral export regulation and management. Conspicuously absent from the list is the use of weapons in a major international war in Europe. The Cold War confrontation did, nevertheless, make great enough demands on western Europe's defence industrial base. And although it proved unnecessary to test the products of Europe's defence industries on home territory, there have been many armed conflicts around the world since 1945 in which weapons of European origin have been used, by European and other forces. At the time of writing this study, events in former Yugoslavia also warn against any complacency in this regard. This chapter begins by explaining how west European states became involved in the import, manufacture and export of major conventional weapons after 1945. The second part of the chapter shows how, during the Cold War, these same states were drawn into various initiatives to regulate the trade in which they had developed such expertise. This chapter stops short of examining the effect on arms export regulation of the Maastricht Treaty and the Common Foreign and Security Policy, which are discussed in Chapter 5.

Import, manufacture and export of major weapons systems

Large-scale imports of arms into western Europe began during the Second World War. Under its March 1941 Lend-Lease Act the US government supplied great quantities of naval, military and air-force weapons and equipment to Britain to support the war against Germany. During its four-and-a-half years of operation the Lend-Lease scheme provided Britain with some $27 billion of military and other goods.[1] Lend-Lease came to an abrupt end in the summer of 1945, but it was not long before the exigencies of the emerging Cold War, combined with large surpluses of military equipment lying idle in the United States, led to the supply chains being restored. Shortly after the enunciation of the Truman Doctrine, in May 1947, the US Congress passed the Greek and Turkish Aid Act by which supplies of US weapons and equipment were passed to those two countries. The year 1949 saw the passage through Congress of the Mutual Defense Assistance Act, designed to assist the allies of the United States in the newly formed North Atlantic Treaty Organization (NATO).

The supply of US arms and equipment became a vital issue again after June 1950, following North Korea's invasion of the South. Convinced that the action in the Far East was the precursor to Soviet aggression in western Europe, a programme of rapid and comprehensive rearmament began, a great proportion of which involved assistance from the United States under the Military Assistance Program (MAP). MAP aid increased dramatically in the mid-1950s.[2] Although the Korean war ended in 1953, the quality and availability of US equipment were such that western Europe was to remain an important outlet for US arms for many years. The economic and industrial recovery of Europe meant that dependency on US arms and military equipment would not last for ever, yet it was not until the early 1970s that arms exports from 'NATO Europe' began to outstrip arms imports, the majority of which had come from the United States.[3]

The recovery and expansion of Europe's defence industries after the war were not uniform. In France, for example, it was not until the early 1960s that defence industries were able to enter the export market in a convincing way. The Italian and West German defence industries were both restricted by postwar controls, although in the Italian case these were largely removed by about 1951.[4] The Italian industry then expanded rapidly, while remaining closely connected to US defence development and production. West Germany remained under close military occupation until the late 1940s. Key issues such as West German rearmament and the reconstruction of the defence industry were not, however, resolved until October 1954 with the signature of the Modified Brussels Treaty. Protocols III and IV to the Modified Treaty placed quantitative and qualitative restrictions on German arms production, and created a regime under which any agreed production could be closely supervised. Among the many weapons listed were weapons of mass destruction (WMD), artillery, tanks, missiles, warships and military aircraft. By 1984 the controls on the production of conventional weapons had been abolished, although prohibitions on the development of WMD were maintained.[5] The British defence industry had survived the war well, and emerged in a strong position to claim a sizeable market share. With clients in the Middle East, Africa, South and Southeast Asia, Britain enjoyed a prominent role in the world arms market. But British success was not to continue unchallenged for long: 'During the fifties, Britain accounted for 21 per cent of total major weapon exports to developing countries. During the sixties, this share had fallen to 11 per cent.'[6]

The rapid growth of defence industries throughout western Europe also persuaded the United States to seek more sophisticated relationships with European partners. As 'buying off the shelf' from the United States was viewed ever less favourably, it had to turn to licensed production agreements, with the attendant transfer of technology. Aircraft such as the F-104 *Starfighter*, the *Hawk* and the *Bullpup*, and the *Sidewinder* missile are all examples of early agreements for the licensed production of sophisticated military equipment.[7] All this meant that from the 1960s onwards, a 'second tier'[8] of west European manufacturers was able to compete increasingly effectively in the world market. These manufacturers were often somewhat less concerned about East–West politics than the United States, but nevertheless generally remained within the broad parameters of Cold War politics.[9] During the late 1960s the leading west European arms exporters (France, the Federal Republic of Germany, Italy, the Netherlands and the UK) secured approximately 10 per cent of the global conventional arms market.[10] In the early 1970s, the picture was complicated by OPEC oil-price rises and the huge demand for weapons in the Middle East. By now the global arms market was also seeing the 'indigenization' of weapons production and export among previous recipients such as Israel, India, Brazil and South Africa, largely as a result of licensed production and other offset arrangements. Nevertheless, the same west European exporters took an increasing share of the growing world arms market. From less than 8 per cent in 1971, the European share had almost doubled by 1975 and subsequently rose to over one-quarter of the world total by 1980.[11] By the early 1980s arms exports had become a vital source of income for Europe's defence industries, with some 70 per cent of Italian conventional arms production being exported, 50 per cent for France, 42 per cent for the UK and 20 per cent for the FRG.[12] In some cases, these exports were to prove controversial; between 1987 and the imposition of the arms embargo in 1991, France alone supplied over 16 per cent of Iraq's weapons imports.[13]

Regulation of arms exports during the Cold War

The period between 1945 and the end of the Cold War not only saw European defence industries achieve and maintain a convincing role in world arms trade, it also saw European governments follow a 'trend towards government control of arms exports' which had been developing in the interwar years.[14] In the 1990s it may seem axiomatic that governments should wish to supervise and regulate the arms trade, and in historical terms it has been the norm for governments to do so.[15] Europe has, however, dallied with *laissez-faire* approaches to the arms trade, particularly in the late nineteenth century and in the years before the First World War,[16] and there are still occasional voices arguing that the arms trade is like any other commercial sector and should therefore not be subject to peculiar intervention by governments. Regulatory efforts were both formal and informal, ranging from arms trade embargoes to transparency initiatives. Activity also took place on many levels, from the UN down to *ad hoc* cooperation among governments. At the bottom of this pyramid of activity is the development of humble national export controls, without which, arguably, none of the larger multilateral initiatives could have been attempted.

Unilateral arms export controls

Several European governments, such as those of France, Italy and Britain, had begun to develop formal national export control systems during the 1930s. The concept of national control was therefore well established by the time the war ended in 1945 and other west European governments began to introduce their own systems. These national systems often shared certain features, including some or all of the following:

- a list of weapons and goods, the export of which required a special licence;
- a list of 'target' countries, either proscribed or preferred;
- a list of criteria or standards against which applications to export might be judged;

- a licence-application procedure and a bureaucracy to enable interdepartmental consultation;
- a method by which licence grants and denials could be verified and policed nationally, a customs service at frontiers and ports, and a set of penalties and the means to impose them;
- a method to guarantee the 'end-use', or non-re-export of the licensed and exported consignment to a destination which would otherwise not have been licensed.

There were, however, important differences across the range of national systems, reflecting different legal and constitutional practices and foreign policy expectations. The pursuit of rigorous national export control policies was sometimes more declaratory than real, particularly among governments which promoted arms exports through special governmental offices and provided 'soft loans' and export credit guarantees. Differences in the scope and quality of national export controls became firmly established; in 1991 the European Commission carried out a survey of national export control systems throughout the EC and discovered that, more than four decades after the supposed renaissance of west European export controls, systems were far from uniform and in some cases standards were extremely low.[17] In spite of the development of elaborate national systems, and in spite of the growing public debate, the export of arms from western Europe since 1945 has been characterized less by restraint than by commercial opportunity-seeking – an observation which begs obvious questions about the sincerity and/or effectiveness of arms export control systems. In some cases, national controls have been simply inadequate for the task. In most other cases, the system has been framed in such a way as to leave the government concerned with the maximum flexibility and the minimum of binding, legislative commitment. The current policy of the British government, for example, is to judge export applications 'on a case by case basis in the light of established criteria'.[18] The FRG, often cited as having the most restrictive approach to arms exports, recently relaxed its rules for weapons exports in order to 'fall in line with emerging European standards for arms exports'.[19]

International regulation

What can be said of national export controls is that they made it possible for west European governments to participate in some sort of structured, multilateral approach to arms trade control. The most obvious structure lay in the Cold War itself. Although west Europeans are often accused of having had the most pragmatic and commercially oriented approach to arms trading during the Cold War, from the point in the 1960s when European defence industries began to take a global market share through to the end of the Cold War, western arms export practices generally corresponded to the bipolar division of the world. West European arms producers and exporters also subscribed to the Coordinating Committee for Multilateral Export Controls (CoCom). CoCom was established in 1949 as a semi-formal, non-treaty embargo-type arrangement to prevent the export of key technologies and weapons to the Soviet Union and the communist bloc.

But it was not only the Cold War which drove efforts to structure and regulate the postwar international arms trade. European governments participated in mandatory and voluntary UN arms embargoes, such as those against South Africa in the 1960s and 1970s. Several European governments were also involved in early attempts by the UN to bring about an international arms-transfer registration system, an idea which was more or less achieved in December 1991 with the establishment of the UN Conventional Arms Register. European governments also helped to devise normative codes of practice for arms exports. The first attempt, the Tripartite Declaration of May 1950, grew out of concerns about a possible arms race in the Palestine area following the 1947–9 war. Britain, France and the United States agreed to provide Israel and the Arab states with only those arms necessary for internal security, for 'legitimate self-defence' and for the 'defence of the area as a whole'. The declaration was worded against the 'aggressive' use of imported weapons and against the use of such weapons to alter territorial boundaries.[20] If any one of the three parties objected to a given arms order then the order would not be met. The declaration resulted in the establishment of the Near East Arms Coordinating Committee which proved to be 'quite effective in controlling the transfer of arms until 1955 when the Soviet Union negotiated the Czech arms deal with Egypt'.[21]

A rather less positive contribution was made by European states to the US-Soviet Conventional Arms Transfer (CAT) talks held in 1977–8. The CAT talks began as an attempt by the Carter administration to expand upon the strict arms-transfer policies which had been developed in Presidential Directive 13 (PD13) of 17 May 1977. PD13 proposed an imaginative set of ideas and criteria to which US arms export decisions should conform, but it also called for the definition of 'norms of supplier restraint' – the bedrock of what promised to be a sophisticated, effective, multilateral regime aimed at control of the global arms trade by the main suppliers acting in conjunction with the recipients. The talks collapsed in December 1978, partly as a result of disagreements within the Carter administration over the broad character of the initiative, and partly because of superpower sensitivity regarding certain key regions. But west European governments also had some responsibility for the failure. Although the prime aim of the talks was to reach agreement between the United States and the Soviet Union, if the resulting vacuums in the arms trade were not simply to be filled by avaricious Europeans, it made sense to include Europe's arms exporters in the process. The reactions of European governments, when asked whether they could support the US-Soviet initiative, ranged from deep scepticism to inertia; Europe would not join the initiative until it was clear that the Soviet Union was willing to be involved. To some extent, this reflected reasonable caution on the part of the Europeans, whose defence industries would be disproportionately affected by any multilateral restraint agreement.[22] European motives may, however, have been more machiavellian; by directing the United States at the highest fence first, the idea may have been to bring the whole enterprise crashing down.[23] Whatever the real motives of the Europeans, the talks collapsed and the initiative, denied the broad support it needed, became no more than a bilateral arrangement doomed to failure; 'it was a mistake to concentrate so heavily on bilateral talks with the Soviet Union, without a greater involvement on the part of West European suppliers'.[24]

West European regulation

While broader international schemes were being discussed, west European governments were also examining the prospects for more local export-control collaboration. With differing standards and systems of national export controls across western Europe, any multilateral export-control initiative by these countries was bound to encounter difficulties from the outset. Nevertheless, several attempts have been made to set up a multilateral arms export control system within western Europe, with four institutions playing a leading role: the Western European Union (WEU), the European Parliament, the European Commission and the European Political Cooperation process (EPC). At the simplest level, some degree of information exchange and transparency, and even commonality in arms export control policies, was considered essential if the WEU's arms stockpile management schemes were to be achieved. It was also thought necessary to create a general sense of confidence in the efficacy of national and international arms embargoes, confidence which would be eroded if European neighbours simply overlooked or were unable to enforce the embargo. Since the 1960s concern had been mounting over the effect of arms exports on the stability of Third World recipients and on the growth of Third World debt, and so it was also thought prudent to ensure that self-denial would not simply open a market opportunity for a less scrupulous European competitor. More recently, there have been calls for tighter, even supranational, west European arms export control policies. The Single European Market with its customs-free trading area prompted demands for a common policy on exports within the EC, and a Community-wide policy on exports of arms outside it.

West European embargoes were imposed against Argentina following the invasion of the Falkland Islands in 1982, against Israel after the invasion of Lebanon in 1982, and against Syria in 1986, after allegations that Syria had been involved in attempting to place explosives on board an Israeli passenger aircraft at a London airport. Europeans have also participated in *ad hoc* multilateral embargoes with non-European partners, such as that imposed by Italy, Belgium, the Netherlands and the United States during the 1967–70 Nigerian civil war. There have also been attempts to make European arms export policies more anticipatory or normative, as in the Modified Brussels Treaty of 1955. The Treaty tried to go far beyond the mere restriction of German arms manufacturing and exports. Protocol IV established the Agency [of the WEU] for the Control of Armaments (ACA). The role of the ACA was not only to police the restrictions on manufacturing set out in Protocol III, but also to control the stocks of key armaments held by each WEU signatory. In order to make the control of such stocks 'effective', it was made clear that the ACA would require control over the production and import of weapons in Europe. Although the activities of the ACA were to be 'confined to the mainland of Europe', and although it was never intended that it should become a central export regulatory body, the preoccupation with stocks of armaments meant that there would have to be some intrusion into member states' export activities, as Article XXII of Protocol IV made clear:

> Each member of the [WEU] shall keep the Agency informed of the quantities of armaments of the types mentioned in Annex IV to Protocol No. III, which are to be exported from its territory on the mainland of Europe. The Agency shall be entitled to satisfy itself that the armaments concerned are in fact exported. If the level of stocks of any item subject to control appears abnormal, the Agency shall further be entitled to enquire into the orders for export.[25]

Although the ACA developed into an elaborate reporting and verification system, the effect on national arms export policies was negligible and it never approximated to a central arms export decision-making body for western Europe. By the mid-1980s the ACA had become more an advisory than a regulatory body.

The ACA initiative did, however, set the scene for a subsequent, rather more ambitious WEU initiative. With growing concern over destabilizing arms sales to the Third World, and with the West seen in some quarters to be capitalizing on the tensions emerging from the process of decolonization, in December 1969 the WEU Committee on Defence Questions and Armaments adopted a draft proposal on the regulation and supervision of the international arms trade.[26] The proposal discussed several ways in which WEU member states could make their arms export decisions more responsible and become involved in international efforts to control the arms trade. Under the WEU initiative, states manufacturing 'major armaments', such as aircraft, missiles, tanks, warships, heavy artillery and radar, would be enjoined not to export such weapons if such exports were judged 'likely to increase the risk of war in any region of the world'. The initiative was, however, inherently discriminatory, in that it did not address the arms traffic 'within the great military alliances'. Although the proposal was adopted by the WEU Assembly, the WEU Council – representing WEU governments – was far less enthusiastic. Providing a foretaste of the European position during the CAT talks of the 1970s, the Council argued that the arrangement could work only with 'the active support of all major supplying countries', and that the views of the recipients would be 'a key factor'.[27] In 1978 another WEU study, the Dankert *Report on Arms Procurement*, claimed that arms exports to the Third World would not be necessary if a fully integrated, self-sustaining European defence market could be created. The Dankert Report thus pointed to a key influence on European defence industries after 1945: the reluctance of governments to surrender their independence in matters of defence and the defence industry. This view, symbolized by governments' continued attachment to Article 223 of the 1958 Treaty of Rome, is discussed more fully below.

The issue of common European defence manufacturing and procurement also brought another parliamentary assembly into the debating arena, but with barely more convincing results. The European Parliament (EP) took an approach similar to the argument for defence industrial rationalization which had already been made by the WEU.[28] The EP argued that a more efficient European market would not only save money and contribute to the European share of the NATO burden, but would also reduce the pressure on European manufacturers to export arms. The EP's first major attempt to address arms sales policies came in 1983 with the Fergusson Report of the Political Affairs Committee.[29] Like the 1978 WEU study, the Fergusson Report looked at the creation of a common European defence market and manufacturing base. But the report also addressed the issue of arms exports more directly. The report noted that although any 'international system of guidelines' on arms exports would need the support of the United States and the Soviet Union, efforts by the EC would nevertheless be an 'important step'. It recommended a return to the CAT talks of the 1970s, with European participation, and supplier/ recipient talks in 'precarious' regions. The report called upon governments to 'establish rules governing the export of arms from Member States to third countries', called for restrictions on the export of certain types of weapons (to be specified), and recommended a continual review process.[30]

Commenting on the Fergusson Report, the EP Committee on External and Economic Affairs went further and called for a 'European Convention against arms exports' which would have to be developed under the auspices of the intergovernmental EPC process, noting that 'it is scarcely conceivable that the Community could be given responsibility for matters relating to arms exports, which are closely linked with the foreign policies of individual countries, until a common foreign policy has been formulated'.[31] The Committee proposed an export control system based on an exclusive 'standard list' of preferred countries, and a 'European arms exports control agency which would supply information on arms exports'.[32] The Committee made three recommendations to the EP. The first of these, the rather anodyne recommendation that arms exports to the Third World be reduced, was carried in plenary. The EP did not, however, support the second and third recommendations: that an EC policy on arms exports should be adopted and that a European arms exports control agency should be established. Issues such as these were debated heatedly at Strasbourg, with a vigour which reflected a basic lack of consensus among European governments, resulting in 'little subsequent implementation'.[33]

In 1986, with the passage of the Single European Act (SEA), it appeared that the major obstruction noted in the Fergusson Report was weakening. The main purpose of the SEA was, in the words of Article 8A of the EEC Treaty, to programme the development of 'an internal market comprising an area without internal frontiers in which the free movement of goods, persons, services and capital is ensured'. The removal of intra-EC customs barriers would have an immediate effect on national arms export controls. It was also realized that the Single European Market (SEM) could have a more general effect on the defence industry, particularly if national practices in the defence sector threatened to undermine the overall aim of common industrial policies and practices. However, while the timetable for the SEM was new, the underlying principles were familiar; arguments for extending Community competence into defence manufacturing and procurement had been made in the late 1970s and early 1980s, when the Fergusson Report was being prepared.[34] The distinguishing feature of the SEA, as far as arms export policies were concerned, was that it seemed to offer greater integration in foreign and security policies, the absence of which had been noted as a major drawback by the Fergusson Report. This inspired the EP's next major review of the arms trade. In February 1987 the Political Affairs Committee commissioned another study which was eventually tabled at the EP on 22 February 1989 as the Ford Report.[35]

The Ford Report argued that the SEM would provide 'an opportunity to move towards common weapons procurement and to reduce the dependence of Community manufacturers on the export trade'.[36] An efficient and 'effective' common European defence market would enable manufacturers to amortize research and development costs and achieve economies of scale without exporting weapons: 'the rationalisation of the European armaments sector by means of armaments cooperation will reduce the necessity to export arms'.[37] But the report recognized that there could be no certainty that a more efficient European defence sector would lose its interest in arms exports, particularly since the Independent European Programme Group (IEPG) clearly viewed increased efficiency as the precursor to more successful export bids.[38] In order to prevent a more efficient European industry simply competing for a larger share of the world market, and in order to hedge against the use of other arguments – such as defence-industry unemployment – to justify arms exports, the report saw that a political consensus would be required. The newly institutionalized EPC seemed to offer the opportunity to achieve just such a consensus. The report claimed that the SEA 'prevent[ed] member states from taking any action which would endanger the security of the countries of the [EC]' and inferred that since arms exports 'could endanger European security' they could 'legitimately be regulated by the Community'.[39] The report called for a 'common arms sales policy' to be developed through EPC based on the following principles:

- the security interests of the [EC];
- the state of democracy of a potential recipient country;
- its real need and the potential purpose of the purchase of armaments;
- its respect of human and civil rights;
- its ability to pay without damaging the internal economy too much;
- the need to limit countertrade because of its distorting effect on world trade.[40]

But the stumbling block was the question of how any Community competence in defence-related matters could be allocated and controlled. The report called on the Commission to 'clarify the interpretation of Article 223 of the Treaty of Rome and Title III of the Single Act as regards the development of a Common Arms Market in Europe'.[41]

Since the 1958 Treaty of Rome (EEC), the pursuit of integrated policies in arms manufacturing, procurement and export has been impeded by the reluctance of the main European arms producers to accept a central EC role in matters of defence. The 'high politics' of national security were the special preserve of sovereign national governments and were not to be subsumed into any civil commercial and industrial integration taking place in the 'common market'. NATO was the central defence alliance and any collaboration in the European context was to take place within the limited, intergovernmental confines of EPC. Since the SEA implicitly denied the possibility of collaboration in the 'military' aspects of security, the point at issue was whether European defence industrial policy and procurement, and by extension certain aspects of arms exports, could come under the rubric 'political and economic'. By allowing member states to derogate from EC competition rules on the grounds of national security, Article 223 has been a major obstacle in the way of the extension of Community competence into defence-related areas: 'The Single Market notwithstanding, as long as Article 223 ... remains unchanged, the EC Commission cannot hope to gain full control over the European arms market.'[42] Article 223 reads as follows:

1. The provisions of this Treaty shall not preclude the application of the following rules:
   (a) No Member State shall be obliged to supply information the disclosure of which it considers contrary to the essential interests of its security;
   (b) Any Member State may take such measures as it considers

necessary for the protection of the essential interests of its
security which are connected with the production of or trade in
arms, munitions and war material; such measures shall not
adversely affect the conditions of competition in the common
market regarding products which are not intended for specifically military purposes.

2. During the first year after the entry into force of this Treaty, the
Council shall, acting unanimously, draw up a list of products to
which the provisions of paragraph 1(b) shall apply.

3. The Council may, acting unanimously on a proposal from the
Commission, make changes in this list.

In a sense, therefore, the Ford Report issued a challenge to the Commission and member governments to clarify precisely where EC
supranational authority ended and national sovereignty began. Previously, the Commission had 'tended to hold back' on questions related to
arms exports.[43] But in March 1989, possibly emboldened by the recent
publication of the Ford Report, the new Internal Market Commissioner,
Martin Bangemann, called for a Commission role in directing not just
arms production, but also trade, indicating a shift in the terms of debate.[44]
The Commission has continued to argue against the segregation of the
defence sector and has been especially keen to see the suppression, or at
least restrictive application, of Article 223. The development of the dual-
use technology export regulation, a good example of a clash between
cautious governments and an ambitious Commission, is discussed in
Chapter 3, while Chapter 5 reviews the current controversy surrounding
the extension of Community competence into defence-related areas.

Europe after the Cold War

From autumn 1989, the context in which thinking about European
defence industry and arms exports had so far taken place did not so much
alter as disappear. The ending of the Cold War set the agenda for change.
But it was the Gulf War of 1990–91 which prompted the members of the
EC to seek new ways to control arms transfers. Some of Iraq's major
arms suppliers were EC members, and in some cases European troops in
the US-led coalition faced Iraqis wielding high-specification weaponry
which had been exported from Europe. After the war, as the UN
organized a series of inspections of Iraqi weapons research and manufacturing facilities, it also became clear that several EC states had supplied,

knowingly or otherwise, weapons-related technology to Iraq. The handling of the Iraq/Kuwait crisis was portrayed in some quarters as proof of the inadequacy of EC foreign policy cooperation in the more loosely ordered post-Cold War world. This perception contributed to the review of EC foreign and security policy-making which had been under way since December 1990 in the Intergovernmental Conference on Political Union (IGC[PU]). With Europe's defence industries increasingly reliant on weapons exports, with some sense of responsibility for having allowed Saddam Hussein to build up what the UN and others considered to be a 'destabilizing and excessive' collection of weapons and technology, and with calls to review and tighten foreign and security policy cooperation, the debate in western Europe developed rapidly.

The main participants in the EC debate remained the Commission, the Parliament and the member states through the EPC process. The Commission continued its campaign to scrap Article 223, particularly in the context of the dual-use regulation. The EP moved quickly to join and influence the debate. On the day the Berlin Wall was breached, 9 November 1989, the EP's Political Affairs Committee asked permission to report on the development of a European security policy. The report was drafted during 1990 and published in April 1991 as the *Report on the Outlook for a European Security Policy*, also known as the Poettering Report.[45] Noting that the SEA stipulated that the EP should be 'associated with the development of a common foreign and security policy', the Poettering Report addressed the European security debate in broad terms and advocated the introduction of an integrated CFSP which would improve upon and 'overcome' the 'intergovernmental character of EPC'.[46] As far as defence industrial cooperation and arms transfers were concerned, the report supported the immediate deletion of Article 223 from the EEC Treaty, called upon the Commission to consider creating a 'special independent agency', the purpose of which would be to 'monitor and control the production and sale of arms in the Member States, among themselves and to third countries',[47] and called for a 'common policy on controlling arms exports' encompassing 'common standards', 'effective monitoring' and 'reduced dependence on exports to third countries'.[48]

The outcome of the IGC(PU) fell somewhat short of the expectations of the Poettering Report, both generally and in terms of arms exports. Undeterred, the EP returned to the debate in September 1992 with a much firmer resolution on arms exports.[49] The EP threatened 'utmost disapproval if new arms markets are sought in Third World countries in order to offset arms cuts in Europe' and called for 'matters pertaining to armaments production and the arms trade' to be 'brought within the Community ambit in anticipation of European Union'. Reflecting a sentiment shared in some capitals, the resolution also argued that extension of the Community's competence in these fields would be 'the first plank in the Common Foreign Security Policy (CFSP)'. The resolution insisted that a 'strict common arms production policy' and a 'common market in arms' would 'help save costs and reduce arms exports to Third World countries'.[50] Arms exports should take account of the 'sufficiency principle': 'Member States should undertake coordinated steps with a view to cutting off supplies of war material to third countries whose military capability is sufficient for their own defence'.[51] The September 1992 resolution was particularly ambitious regarding arms transfer controls and the role of the EP in decision-making. Among informal official reactions to the resolution, the view that it was 'a good job we can afford to ignore the EP' was not untypical, and the impression given by newspaper headlines such as 'EC nations vote for controls on weapons exports' proved to be exaggerated.[52]

The main forum for action on conventional arms exports remained the EPC process, up to the entry into force of the Maastricht Treaty in 1993. Interest did not simply begin with the commencement of the IGC(PU) in December 1990, however. In the summer of 1989, a Political Committee working group was convened to examine the problems which the SEM might pose for national arms export controls. The Dutch floated the idea of using a Benelux-style system, where the original supplier's export policies and licences would be honoured throughout the Community. Little real progress was made, however, until spring 1991, following the expulsion of Iraqi forces from Kuwait.

In March 1991 the Political Committee agreed that another *ad hoc* group of experts should meet to consider coordination of national policies on conventional arms exports and definitions of arms embargoes. The first meeting of this new body – the Ad Hoc Working Group on Conventional Arms Exports – took place on 16 April 1991. The group's first tasks were to compare national positions and investigate the possibility of further action. Already, differences were emerging between those member states such as Britain and France which sought to limit the process to a comparison of national lists of controlled military goods, drawn up in addition to CoCom's munitions list, and those such as Germany which sought to integrate national policies, seeing such a process as a 'springboard' to an eventual CFSP. The first fruits of the comparison of national practices was the statement made in June 1991 after the Luxembourg European Council, listing seven criteria for conventional arms exports found to be common to the member states. These criteria, along with the eighth which was agreed at the Lisbon European Council twelve months later, are reproduced in the Appendix. At Luxembourg, rather than use the language of 'common policy' and integration, the Council was merely hopeful that a 'common approach' based on 'criteria of this nature' might lead to 'a harmonization of national policies'.[53] It was stressed at the time, and repeatedly since, that several governments did not consider the criteria to be the first steps towards a common policy on arms exports, nor was there a commitment that all criteria would be 'applied' in all cases.

Technical experts also met during summer 1991 to discuss a 'Common Reference List' (CRL) of weapons and military items, to the export or transfer of which the common criteria might be applied. Other meetings addressed arms embargo policies and practice, and a comparison was made of export licensing procedures to see where they could be aligned. The 'Review of Existing EC and UN Embargoes with a View to Joint Action on Implementation' was concluded on 8 July 1991 when the Political Committee endorsed the group's proposal for a four-level 'menu of options' for arms embargoes:

- Level 1: weapons designed to kill and their ammunition;
- Level 2: weapons platforms;
- Level 3: non-weapons platforms;
- Level 4: ancillary equipment.

Over the following months the *ad hoc* group worked on four main areas: comparison of the lists of goods to which partners applied their conventional arms export policies, and the development of the CRL; comparison of the employment of end-use certificates and non-re-exportation clauses; a survey of national procedures for the revocation of export licences; and a comparison of practices concerning commercial and industrial negotiations, the signature of conventional arms export contracts, and the control of production, storage and transport of conventional arms prior to their export. Fine-tuning has continued ever since. There was also, within the *ad hoc* group, some discussion about the effect of the SEM, in particular whether the internal market would result in less effective ex-Union export controls. But the problem was essentially procedural rather than legal or in terms of competence, since Article 223 was still very clearly in force. This seemed to be of particular concern in mid-December 1992, when the group agreed on a system of interim documentation to deal with intra-Union arms exports while a 'Standardised Accompanying Document' was being devised.

While the EPC was examining the coordination of conventional arms export policies, the IGC(PU) continued its work, culminating in the Treaty on European Union (TEU), or Maastricht Treaty, in December 1991. The TEU entered into force in November 1993 and the 'three-pillared' European Union came into being. The EPC process was replaced by the Common Foreign and Security Policy. CFSP remained, however, an intergovernmental affair, differing from EPC principally in the sense that foreign and security policy cooperation was given a more formal base in the Union Treaty, and in the sense that CFSP went beyond the 'political and economic' aspects of security policy claimed by the SEA to embrace 'all questions related to the security of the Union, including the eventual framing of a common defence policy, which might in time lead to a common defence'.[54] The continued preference for intergovernmentalism was seen both in the retention of Article 223 and in the carefully crafted CFSP voting process known as 'joint action'. CFSP, and the joint-action process, are examined in more detail in Chapter 5, but it is appropriate at this point to examine the manner in which arms exports came to be a candidate for the process, not least because the outcome may have been the result of bureaucratic confusion.

The TEU makes plain, in Article J.1.1, that CFSP is to cover 'all areas of foreign and security policy'. Although security policy logically embraces questions of defence policy and the creation of a 'common defence', an impression supported by the wording of Article J.4.1,[55] Article J.4.3 indicates that issues with 'defence implications' would not be appropriate for the closer forms of cooperation being made available under CFSP. In effect, CFSP and the joint-action process were to be confined to non-defence security issues and foreign policy issues, with the latter being thought to offer the best possibilities for developing more intimate intergovernmental cooperation through joint action. Ultimately, however, various *security* issues were listed as potential candidates for joint action, rather than 'softer' foreign policy-type issues. In the approach to the Maastricht European Council, governments had been attempting to draw up two lists, one of security issues which might be appropriate for CFSP, and another of foreign policy issues which might be suitable for joint action. In the end, the foreign policy issues were thought too sensitive for joint actions and were deleted. This left a list of security issues known as the 'Asolo List' which, although more sensitive than the foreign policy issues, were then listed as candidates for joint action.[56] The mistake was soon realized and resulted in the 'Declaration on Areas which could be the Subject of Joint Action' not being published with other Treaty documentation. Instead, governments were invited to spend more time discussing subjects for the joint-action process. In June 1992 the Lisbon European Council created an Ad Hoc Working Group on Security under the auspices of the Political Committee, with a mandate to prepare a report on possible areas for joint action for the Edinburgh European Council. The working group held its first meeting on 23 September 1992 in London during the UK Presidency and eventually forwarded its report to the Political Committee in Brussels at the beginning of December. The handling and publication of the report caused some disagreement. Those member states which had yet to ratify the Union Treaty were sensitive to anything which might interrupt ratification. Others were more aggressive and demanded that the report and its conclusions be published. In the end, after threats to leak the report to the media if it were not published, it was agreed to publish the report in full with the conclusions of the Edinburgh European Council, 7–8 December 1992. The Ad Hoc Group had examined the subject in three broad categories:

- 'Areas suitable for joint action by the Union as from the entry into force of the Union Treaty';
- 'Wider issues which the Union will need to address in the course of developing common policies in the security field';
- 'Adjustments to the structure of working groups under the Political Committee which will enable the work under [the two categories] above to be taken forward'.

The object of the report was to build upon the results of EPC and to develop those areas where member states were already working together. In an attempt to water down the commitment to use the joint-action process in security-related areas, the list of issues consisted 'largely of areas in which the Community and its member states are adopting a common approach, or which, based on the experience of [EPC], seem to have the potential for such action'. The report listed four sets of issues which might be suitable for joint action: the CSCE process, disarmament and arms control in Europe, non-proliferation of WMD and economic aspects of security. The CSCE process offered little scope for joint action on arms exports, except insofar as the CSCE's Forum for Security Cooperation was developing a position on conventional arms exports, to which the Union might contribute. The second and third areas offered no additional grounds for joint action on conventional arms exports, but under 'economic aspects of security' there were various transparency and cooperation measures which appeared to offer the possibility of tighter cooperation in matters related to arms exports.

Other than the continuing harmonization of national commodity lists, the development of a standardized accompanying document for intra-EU arms exports and the resolution of certain legal problems regarding the application of the four-level embargo, little further work has been done on the development of integrated arms export policies within the institutions of the EU. The eight criteria have not been adopted or implemented in any formal sense by the EU or the member governments. This is not surprising, given that the criteria were the result of a comparative rather than a policy-making exercise. There have, nevertheless, been two developments which will serve to conclude this chronology of west European involvement in the defence trade, and its regulation. Since late 1992, prompted by the Saferworld organization, the EP has been pressing for the implementation of a 'Code of Conduct' in conventional arms exports based on the eight criteria. A Saferworld report called for the EC to 'act quickly and achieve a high degree of harmonization', particularly in view of the imminence of the SEM. The report recommended that the eight criteria be applied on a sliding scale from the most serious level of an 'international crime of state', to a 'violation of international obligations', to situations where 'arms export restraints might be politically prudent or morally desirable, but where their adoption would clearly be in excess of what is demanded in international law'. In addition, Saferworld recommended a four-level categorization of arms destinations, with exports to those countries listed in 'Group 4' being 'completely banned'.[57]

As well as inspiring the UN General Assembly to call for a worldwide Code of Conduct, the report contributed to a revival of EP interest in arms exports. In January 1995 a 'Resolution on the Need for European Controls on the Export or Transfer of Arms' called for a 'coherent and comprehensive arms control policy on the Union level'. With the 1996 IGC on the horizon, the EP called for the new policy to be included in the CFSP and for Article 223 to be abolished. A 'European Agency for the control of arms exports' was to be investigated and member states were asked to work towards establishing an 'international code of conduct on the control of arms transfers and exports'.[58] A 'European Code of Conduct', based on work by Saferworld and endorsed by 40 European nongovernmental organizations, was launched in Brussels on 11 May 1995 with the endorsement of the EP. Finally, the fact that on 1 January 1995 the European Union accepted three more members has also affected the terms of debate. The addition of Swedish, Finnish and Austrian arms exporters will result in no more than a negligible increase in the EU share of the world arms market. These countries may, however, make their presence felt more clearly in the political debate surrounding the development of common arms export policies. Although not regarded as having loose export policies, Sweden in particular is known to have a robust view of the place of defence industry in national security and would be reluctant to see the removal of Article 223.

Chapter 3

Technology

Introduction

National arms export control systems began to be developed during the 1930s, and many west European countries had some form of supervisory and regulatory mechanism in place by the end of the Second World War. Following the war, these relatively new ideas of export control were applied to technology as well as to weapons. The war had demonstrated on several occasions the strategic benefits to be gained from exploiting new technology, and the risks of allowing an adversary to gain the technological upper hand. Ever since a premium had been placed on straight branches of yew from which bows could be made, and for as long as armourers have had a marketable vocation, both the materials and the 'know-how' for weapon design and manufacture have been prized assets. But the Second World War also showed that strategic advantage was no longer solely a matter of bigger and better weapons. To be sure, Second World War technology had produced guided cruise and ballistic missiles and, of course, the atomic bomb. But radar surveillance and tracking, radio jamming, secure communications systems and rudimentary 'code-cracking' computers were all important examples of the strategic significance of 'harmless' technology. In addition to operations on land and sea, the Second World War also confirmed the strategic value of air power. And by the middle of the twentieth century, the strategic potential of outer space, the deepest oceans and the invisible electromagnetic spectrum were also being investigated. In all this, the microchip was to become for the Cold War what the machine-gun and tank had been for the trench warfare of 1914–18. A 'silent revolution' in warfare had begun, whereby 'superiority over the enemy' would be obtained 'by *qualitative* means'.[1]

With the concept of governmental export control but a few years old, the challenge of the postwar years was to control the traffic not just in weapons but also in related technology. In time, 'related technology' came to mean three different things: the technology used to make weapons; the technology used to make militarily useful equipment such as radars; and the technology which could have both military and innocent civilian applications and which became known as 'dual-use'. As the Cold War progressed, it was dual-use technology which was to cause the biggest political, organizational and commercial difficulties: 'One of the key features of machine tools is versatility. A lathe or a milling machine can be configured to produce parts for a car or a military personnel carrier, parts for a domestic appliance or a rifle ... any competent engineer could [make] the adjustments necessary to turn out military products.'[2]

This chapter is concerned with the development of technology export control systems by the members of the EU. As with the control of arms exports, the foundation of any multilateral technology export control initiative must be effective national instruments. The first part of this chapter therefore looks briefly at the character of national technology export control mechanisms and compares US and west European systems. For most of the period since 1945, most west European governments have practised multilateral export controls not through one of the institutions of the European Community/Union, but in CoCom, the origins, procedures and prospects of which are summarized in the second part of this chapter. The final part of the chapter turns to the development of the EU dual-use regulation.

National export controls

A number of surveys, commercial and academic, have been made of national export control systems, including those of established and new member states of the EU.[3] At an official level, the individual member states of the EU and the European Commission have all been involved in comparisons of national practices and in attempts to 'harmonize' those practices around a mutually acceptable character and standard of control. The various surveys show that all members of the EU now have an elaborate national control structure. In many cases, particularly rapid improvements have been made in the past four or five years, often in response to arms and technology trade scandals exposed during the 1980s. Allegations of improper behaviour by governments and individuals continued to be made into the 1990s, causing significant political instability for a number of EU governments. As a Commission survey made clear in 1991, complex multilateral export control regimes can only be as good as the national systems on which they depend.

The essential features of an export control system were summarized in Chapter 2: a list of controlled commodities; a list of proscribed (or preferred) destinations; a set of export criteria or guidelines; a licensing process and bureaucracy; an enforcement system; and, finally, some provision to prevent re-export or unauthorized 'end-use'. The surveys mentioned above show that the outlines of a common approach had already been adopted by EU members in all these key areas, some time before the formal implementation of the EU dual-use regulation on 1 July 1995. Most sets of national export criteria, for example, referred to the supplier's international obligations, including the enforcement of embargoes, the question of tension, conflict and even war in the country or region of destination, and the customer's record in terms of human rights. As far as controlling the export of weapon-related and dual-use sensitive technology was concerned, most national systems within the EU enforced the lists of technologies already agreed in the Nuclear Suppliers Group (NSG), the Australia Group (AG) and the Missile Technology Control Regime (MTCR). On the industrial dual-use side, most systems either replicated or followed closely the lists of goods set out in CoCom's Industrial List. But even decades of cooperation in CoCom failed to ensure complete uniformity, particularly in the important areas of implementation and enforcement.[4] Some EU members had a preferred country list, while others identified proscribed destinations. Some admitted to having a list of proscribed destinations, but refused to make the list public. Some included among their criteria the economic health of the client and its 'defensive sufficiency'. These proved, however, to be minor differences relative to the high degree of commonality which obtained, at least in organizational terms, and which made possible the development of the EU's multilateral technology export control initiative.

For the purposes of this study four features of European national export control systems, illustrated in the various surveys, merit particular attention. First, parliamentary involvement in export controls is very limited, where it exists at all. At most, national legislatures can expect notification of export decisions and deliveries after the event. In general, policies and decisions regarding sensitive exports remain the preserve of the executive branch of government. National executives may, with some reluctance, be willing to surrender certain of these functions to a central European organization, and may be willing to share their export decision-making process with other EU partners. But in the current climate it seems unlikely that involvement could be extended to the EU's own democratic organ – the European Parliament – when it has not yet been extended to national parliaments. The second feature is that the recently expanded EU now has four members (Austria, Finland, Ireland and Sweden) which have traditions of non-alignment during peace and neutrality during war. This could have two implications for the development of common European policies in defence-related manufacturing and export. Particularly in Austria and Sweden, the policies of non-alignment and neutrality have implied independence of foreign suppliers of defence equipment. This in turn has led to the development of strong national defence industries. With a national mind-set that supports the development and maintenance of a national defence sector, it might be expected that defence exports, without which any national defence industry would be in difficulties, would be viewed through the same prism. These same countries might also, for historical and cultural reasons, balk at attempts to ally European defence exports with common European foreign, security and, particularly, defence policies.

The third feature to note is the variation in attitudes to Article 223 of the 1958 EEC Treaty. Article 223 remains, for some, the final obstacle to full-scale EU cooperation in all matters relating to defence manufacturing and export, although some new member states such as Finland appear to have little interest in the fate of Article 223; Finland is, after all, a minor manufacturer and exporter of weaponry. Germany, a rather more significant exporter of military equipment and sensitive technology, favours the abandonment of Article 223 in favour of a fully harmonized, EU-wide 'single policy' in arms exports, one which would be less restrictive than current national policies. On the other hand, Britain and France, both large-scale exporters of defence-related equipment and weapons, would not be willing to abandon the protection, as they view it, which Article 223 offers against over-restrictive and intrusive central EU policies. To complicate the picture, Sweden – a significant exporter but with a tradition of neutrality – shares the British and French view that Article 223 should be retained, but only in order to prevent the EU applying common export control standards which could be lower than those currently applied by Sweden.

The final feature is the relationship between government and industry. Industry generally has little if any formal involvement in the development of national export control policies. In many EU member states, little effort is made to include industry even on an information-only basis, although some governments do go to great lengths to communicate policies and changes to industry. Some member states, though not all, require exporters to nominate a company board member or executive to administer export control compliance and to accept responsibility for breaches. Differences across the EU in the government/industry relationship can also be seen in the extent to which industry is expected to police itself. The 'catch-all' clause of the EU regulation is discussed more fully below; what might be said at this point is that the notion that industry can be made to have an open-ended responsibility for the failure of export controls can present legal and constitutional difficulties for several member states and may create legal conflicts within the EU. Britain and Germany, for example, both employ catch-all provisions, although the precise understanding and meaning of the expression differs in each case; in Germany, catch-all clauses come into effect if the exporter has 'positive knowledge' of intended misuse, but in Britain the catch-all or 'end-use' clause operates not only when an exporter 'knows', but also when he has 'grounds for suspecting' that a given export might be misused.[5] In the British official view, the exporter carries a high degree of responsibility:

> generally the initial responsibility for determining the need for a licence under the 'end-use' control will rest with you [the exporter]. You know the capabilities of your products, your customers and potential customers and the circumstances of any particular order far better than Government officials.[6]

The British approach does not, however, find unqualified support around the EU; an official of one of the newest member governments described the catch-all as 'totalitarian'.

Germany in fact operates two catch-all clauses; one relating to conventional weapons production and one to nuclear matters. Germany's policy is exceptional in that many other national catch-all clauses, as well as the appropriate clause of the EU regulation, refer only to weapons of mass destruction.[7] Although WMD non-proliferation is not covered in this study, the catch-all is relevant in that it represents an attempt to employ export control practices which originate in, and are appropriate for, the United States, but which are alien to government/industry relationships in Europe. The catch-all appeared in US legislation in December 1990 in the form of the 'Enhanced Proliferation Control Initiative' (EPCI). The EPCI imposed new licensing requirements in order to prevent the proliferation of chemical and biological weaponry and related technology and materials. The initiative stated that a licence would henceforth be required in a number of circumstances, including 'If a US person knows that a proposed export or other assistance is destined for CBW or missile activities in listed regions, countries, or projects.'[8] The EPCI is in keeping with a long tradition in the US of export controls, a tradition in which the executive branch of government has accrued immense, almost absolute authority to limit trade – both general and military-related – for reasons of national security or foreign policy, even to the extent of conducting general 'economic warfare'. The US International Traffic in Arms Regulations, for example, allow the Office of Defense Trade Controls of the State Department to suspend, revoke or deny any licence without prior notice. The general character of postwar US export controls dates from the 1949 Export Control Act, passed in the context of rapidly deteriorating East-West relations:

> Two important principles were embodied in the 1949 legislation and have survived virtually intact through multiple revisions. First, the executive branch was to enjoy broad authority to determine what products or technical data should be subject to export licensing, to administer the licensing system, and to impose penalties for violations. Second, the rule-making process, including the composition of the control list, was (and continues to be) largely exempt from the usual process of public comment and virtually immune from judicial review.[9]

Thus, the export from the United States of almost any good, from tanks to toys, along with the relevant hard, soft and intangible technology, requires official approval. For the vast majority of exports, the good concerned has no strategic value whatsoever. Nevertheless, the export has still to be approved, usually in the form of a licence which is termed 'open' or 'general', but which is no less a licence. Where the export of weapons or sensitive technology is concerned, even a relaxation of controls can be made only by issuing a new licence; when, in April 1994, the Clinton administration sought to allow US exporters to supply low-level dual-use technology to the former Soviet Union and the People's Republic of China, without first seeking government approval, the method chosen was to issue a new, general licence. At the time, this concession was described as a 'key change in US export licensing procedures',[10] but the incident also illustrates the importance placed in the United States on licensing and government control. Although the Clinton administration has sought to reduce the burden of individual licensing, especially with regard to civilian telecommunications equipment and certain computers, the US export control system is still largely 'commodity-based' rather than 'destination-based', and in these circumstances there remains a blanket presumption that exports should be regulated.[11] Tight government control of exports from the US means that trade restrictions and embargoes can be switched on and off rapidly and relatively simply and, as noted above, with little or no opportunity for redress offered to industry and the public. The EPCI catch-all, and the fact that US commodity control lists often contain a so-called 'bucket entry' designed to spread the coverage of the lists as widely as possible, are symptomatic of this culture of control. Exports from the United States are in effect a matter of privilege rather than right. In mid-1995 it was proposed that the US export control system be 'entirely reorganized and streamlined' and that licensing requirements be made much more specific.[12] One result of the proposed changes will be to make government-industry relationships more flexible and reasonable. But for the present, US government continues to err on the side of regulation. US industry therefore remains committed to defensive self-regulation and to understanding and complying with government thinking in order to avoid wasting time, effort and money.

In Europe, and in Japan, a different view prevails. Although commodity control lists appear to be very similar to those used in the United States, the underlying presumption in these countries is that export is a right. The right to export is not unlimited, but the burden lies on governments to identify and list sensitive commodities and destinations and it is only within these parameters that industry can be expected to act responsibly and conform. If a proposed export falls outside the listed prohibitions then the responsibility or otherwise of the exporter should not come into question, and the export should proceed. In Europe, the expectation is that export controls should be kept to the minimum necessary. If industry can be expected to be self-policing, in the sense of the catch-all idea, then the reasons for export prohibitions must be reasonable and clearly stated. If the reasons given are imprecise or open-ended, the right to export might be impinged upon unnecessarily and unfairly. The majority of exports from Europe take place without any form of licensing whatsoever, unlike in the United States. General and open licences are used in Europe, but only in order to moderate a licensing system which is regarded as exceptional, rather than as a means to extend nominal control over all exports, as in the United States. Arguably, the introduction into Europe of a tight, US-style regulatory system, along with the catch-all idea which readily follows from it, could help to improve national licensing systems and might then become the basis for a uniform, EU-wide system. But such a step would present fundamental constitutional challenges and would require significant change in the cultural and legal character of industry-government relations in western Europe. In any case, Europe would be importing a model of licensing which its originator was in the process of revising or even abandoning.

Multilateral technology export controls: CoCom and its successor

Postwar attempts at multilateral export control began with the Coordinating Committee for Multilateral Export Controls (CoCom). CoCom was founded in 1949, at the height of the Cold War. Britain and other western states saw that the export of machine tools and other technology to the Soviet Union, while it might be commercially beneficial, could have adverse strategic consequences.[13] CoCom was not a treaty-based arrangement, and its proceedings were not held in the public eye. The organization was based in the US Embassy in Paris, where regular meetings took place and where a permanent Coordinating Group carried out its work.

Sometimes described as the 'economic arm of NATO', CoCom's aim was to restrict the supply of key technology and commodities to Cold War adversaries. The Soviet Union and its satellites, China and other countries all appeared on a 'Country List' of proscribed destinations. In order to prevent diversion of key technology via third countries, CoCom partners also initiated a 'Third Country Cooperation Initiative'. The partners (NATO members less Iceland, plus Japan and, since 1989, Australia) agreed to national enforcement of agreed controls on goods and technologies contained in three commodity lists which were updated every four years. The 'International Munitions List' (IML) covered conventional arms, munitions and items which were unequivocally military, and subsequently formed the basis of the exclusions under Article 223 of the EEC Treaty. The 'International Atomic Energy List' (IAEL) dealt with technology needed for nuclear-weapon design and testing. Finally, the 'International Industrial List' (IIL) included items with dual civil/military use. The IIL covered a huge range of products and technology, including advanced materials such as carbon fibre (which might be used in aircraft production), computer-controlled machine tools and the appropriate software, silicon-based micro-circuitry, high-grade digital and laser telecommunications equipment, optical and sensor systems, navigation technology and other types of marine equipment. From the point of view of Western national and multilateral control of technology transfers, the importance of CoCom cannot be overstated; by one account CoCom was nothing less than 'the principal forum for the Western allies to agree upon and implement restrictions on trade in weapons and dual-use goods and technologies with Soviet-bloc and other Communist countries'.[14] National export controls were heavily influenced by CoCom, and the EU dual-use regulation developed in its shadow.

CoCom was both a tool of economic warfare and a general strategic embargo. It was always a difficult matter of good intelligence and sound judgment to know which goods and technologies contributed to Soviet military capability, and which western industries should therefore suffer restrictions.[15] It was generally accepted that the most CoCom could do was delay the acquisition of leading technologies by the communist bloc, thereby ensuring that the West maintained the technological upper hand. But, in spite of the perceived presence of an overwhelming, unifying military threat to the West, CoCom was never free of controversy and misunderstanding among its partners. Having agreed unanimously on the content of the destination and commodity lists and any amendments, CoCom partners had to seek a 'general exception' if they wished to export a listed good to a proscribed destination. Since an exception could also only be agreed unanimously, this process, known as 'consensus licensing', effectively meant that each partner had a 'right to veto the sales of others'.[16] However, since CoCom was a voluntary organization, the use of the veto was always a delicate matter and had to be balanced 'against the possibility that members may withdraw from the group at any moment without notice'.[17] The key criterion was whether the proposed export would improve the recipient's military capabilities; commodities which appeared on the IAEL or the IML were therefore never approved for export, although those on the IIL were often the cause of dispute. Some partners made use of 'administrative exception notes' by which they stated that certain items would be subjected to national control and would not be made subject to collective review in CoCom and hence vulnerable to a veto.[18]

Although the end of the Cold War brought the rationale for CoCom into question, many continued to argue for a multilateral forum to control the export of sensitive technologies. Partly in response to the expansion of WMD non-proliferation regimes into the dual-use area, and partly to present a more accommodating face to the technology-starved former Soviet Union and its allies, in 1990 CoCom began to reduce its IIL to a 'Core List' of especially sensitive technology.[19] This list was finalized in February 1992, although disagreements remained over controls on certain technologies such as computers and telecommunications.[20] May 1992 saw the creation of an informal CoCom Cooperation Forum, acknowledging that many former Warsaw Treaty states not only needed western technology for their economic stability and could be removed from CoCom's Country List, as was Hungary in February 1992, but also that 'the new strategic threats were the dangers of the spread of weapons of mass destruction to Third World countries'[21] and to terrorist groups.[22] Thus, the idea was born of using CoCom as a general export control mechanism, rather than a more focused, East–West technology embargo or weapon of economic warfare.

At a meeting of CoCom partners at The Hague on 16 November 1993 it was agreed that the forum was now defunct, and that CoCom controls should be phased out by 31 March 1994. On the eve of the organization's demise, however, the partners agreed that a replacement forum should be in place by the end of 1994. For the interim period, partners agreed to maintain the commodity lists – the 'Core List' residue of the IIL became known as the 'Interim List' – while accepting more flexibility and national discretion in the granting of export licences.[23] CoCom was duly wound up on 31 March 1994, while negotiations continued to find an appropriate successor regime. The question of the membership of any new body provoked controversy. Those who saw in the new body a means to manage global dual-use technology and conventional weapons transfers argued that Russia must be made a member of the new organization from the outset, with the PRC and other states also joining eventually. Britain and France, in particular, argued that the new body would have little meaning without Russian membership. Russia's arms sales to Iran became a sticking point. Russia's pledge in September 1994 that it would halt future arms sales to Iran ignored existing contracts to supply top-grade MiG-29 and SU-24 combat aircraft, T-72 main battle tanks and infantry combat vehicles, and failed to convince the United States. It was not until 29 June 1995 that Russia and the United States finally reached a firm agreement. As a result, by midsummer 1995 it was expected that Russia, Poland, Hungary and the Czech Republic would all be invited to join the seventeen original partners and the six cooperating partners (Austria, Finland, Ireland, New Zealand, Sweden and Switzerland) for high-level discussions on CoCom's successor in September 1995.[24]

Even with the membership issue approaching resolution, and having agreed on a provisional title for the new organization (New Forum), there remained deep uncertainty about the basic rationale for the new body. There was general agreement that the new body should cover the export of military and dual-use technologies, but some doubts as to how – or whether – the arrangement could also cover conventional weapons exports. The problem of how to replace CoCom's Country List also led to disagreements. The United States was eager to name the four so-called 'pariah' states (Iran, Iraq, Libya and North Korea) as the main targets of the new regime, but European partners were 'steadfastly against this'.[25] The British Foreign Office described the difficulty facing the negotiators in the following way:

> instead of looking simply at trade with countries that formerly made up the Warsaw Pact, we are now looking at trade with the whole world. In the area of dual use technology where a lot of the members of COCOM are big traders, we have in the negotiations the difficulty of striking a balance between the security desiderata which point to something ... close to the old COCOM system and which gives as much chance to restrict trade as possible and at the other extreme the wish to promote legitimate trade in dual use goods which argues for controls which are focused ... on end users and end uses on which we have concerns, and does not any longer have a kind of blanket effect. What is proving difficult in the negotiations so far is to strike that balance.[26]

Problems also arose in the selection of criteria or guidelines by which partners would judge potential arms and military-equipment exports. According to one British source, by March 1995 there had been 'virtually no progress' in agreeing such guidelines.[27] Discussion of the new regime's consultation process has also revealed deep divisions. The United States has consistently argued for prior notification of impending sales among the partners. But some states felt that this practice would expose their defence companies to price-cutting manoeuvres,[28] and one senior British official described the idea as 'anathema'. What seems more likely is that the national veto will be abandoned, bringing the old 'consensus licensing' process to an end, and that the new regime will, instead, be a looser and more informal arrangement in which national discretion, known as 'administrative exceptions' in CoCom, will predominate. While the emphasis on national judgment and implementation may be a realistic response to political and commercial pressures, it is difficult to see how an effective multilateral control regime could be built upon such unsteady foundations; the stress on national discretion could prove to be a fatal flaw.[29] The pressure to ease export regulations and promote exports is great, particularly in the United States, and could overwhelm the new regime. If the outcome of the post-CoCom negotiations is no more than a loose, toothless 'transparency' agreement among suppliers, this could prove damaging to European manufacturers and exporters of sensitive conventional weapons-related technology. Some European industrialists worry that if the only multilateral regime governing US exports is the post-CoCom arrangement, this could give US industry competitive advantage over European competitors governed by a far more restrictive EU dual-use regulation.

The EU dual-use export regulation

With so many EU members involved both in CoCom and the various WMD technology-control initiatives, there is a great deal of experience of multilateral technology export control within the EU. Nevertheless, it has so far proved difficult to harness that experience in one or other of the Union institutions. From the earliest days, some member states have been particularly sensitive to the issue of Community competence in areas which, although clearly matters of trade and competition, also touch on national foreign, defence and security policies. This situation is partly explained by Article 223 of the 1958 EEC Treaty, discussed in Chapter 2. The list of goods to be covered by Article 223, derived from the CoCom IML, was agreed soon after the EEC Treaty was signed. The list includes conventional weapons such as artillery, tanks, missiles and warships, as well as the ammunition for such weapons, and also mentions nuclear, biological and chemical weapons. Military computers and electronic equipment are included, as well as other military equipment such as parachute fabric and water-purification plants. The final paragraph concerns manufacturing technology which is exclusively military, rather than dual-use: 'Machines, equipment and items exclusively designed for the study, manufacture, testing and control of arms, munitions and apparatus of an exclusively military nature included in this list'.[30]

The list has not been updated since 1958. Many of the weapons have been superseded, and a good deal of modern military equipment is not included. The failure to modernize the list may have suggested to some governments that the principle of exception matters more than the content of the list, with each government being free to decide for itself which commodities are covered by the Article. Some critics have suspected governments of applying Article 223 as loosely as possible to dual-use technology as well as arms and military technology, in order to maintain national competitive advantage within the European market.[31] In fact, the legal ground has long been established that members cannot derogate from Community commercial and industrial policies by citing the military side of dual-use goods. If a good has a civilian use, then the Community has competence, even where dual-use goods are managed by other regimes such as CoCom, the NSG, the AG and the MTCR. In other words, exemption from Article 223 is to be limited as far as possible to the list of military goods and technologies appended to it. Checks against cynical misinterpretation of Article 223 can be found in Articles 224 and 225 of the EEC Treaty, and in Article 223 itself, paragraph 1(b) of which states that any exclusions under the Article 'shall not adversely affect the conditions of competition in the common market regarding products which are not intended for specifically military purposes'. The principle of restricted derogation was reiterated by the Commission after the adoption of the Single European Act.[32] It follows that Community competence extends into all areas not explicitly reserved for national prerogative, including the dual-use goods listed in the CoCom IIL. Article 223 was not amended by the Single European Act, was not scrapped in accordance with Commission proposals,[33] was not rescinded by the Maastricht Treaty in December 1991, and remains a source of controversy.

The Commission first began to examine the issue of export controls on sensitive and dual-use goods in the 1980s. When the Single European Act of 1986 set the date for the beginning of the single market, the export control issue loomed still larger. Given EC members' commitments to the various dual-use export control bodies, especially CoCom, it became apparent that a single market with no internal customs barriers would require a Community-wide policy for the export of sensitive or strategic goods which could not be exempted under Article 223 and which were therefore vulnerable to EC industrial, commercial and competition policies. Unless all EC members had comparable export policies and standards of implementation, licence-free trade in dual-use technology within the single market area could enable unscrupulous exporters to evade controls in their home state by exporting first to a customer in another EC state with more lax controls before re-exporting to the final, perhaps otherwise proscribed, destination. In the longer term, it could also be that states with more lax controls could, unfairly, attract additional investment for the manufacture of dual-use goods. The winding-down of CoCom posed another problem, since those EC members which were also CoCom participants had introduced simplified licensing systems for exports of sensitive goods to other CoCom partners and CoCom cooperation countries.

It was not only the effect of the single market on sensitive export policies which had to be considered, however, but also how such policies might affect the internal management of the single market, where as much as 5 per cent of internal trade is in goods which could be classified as dual-use.[34] The single market requires there to be no internal barriers or idiosyncratic export control systems which might divide the market. However much they agreed with EC common commercial policy, if member states were adamant in their wish to control exports of dual-use technology on grounds of national security, the result could only be anti-competitive practices where the civilian use of the technology or commodity was concerned. Unless controlled dual-use items are traded freely within the EC, without the delays and costs associated with the obtaining of licences, there could be significant barriers to civil trade.

For all these reasons, along with the perception that transnational industrial cooperation could offer less scrupulous companies a means to evade the strongest national restrictions, the long-drawn-out attempt began to fashion a compromise between Community competence in trade matters, and national prerogative in the areas of foreign, security and defence policies. While respecting the Community's competition policies and the aims of the single market, the object of the exercise was to ensure that free and flexible intra-EC trade did not make possible the diversion of sensitive goods to third countries via the weakest link in the EC 'fence'. The first step in the development of an EC/EU dual-use policy was a fact-finding survey of national practices carried out by the Commission in 1991. In a 'communication' to the Council and Parliament, the Commission, referring to the need 'to ensure that export-type controls on intra-EC trade do not hinder the completion of the internal market',[35] listed 'key elements' for 'an operational and effective system at Community level':

- 'a common list of dual-use goods and technologies which are subject to control';
- 'a common list of destinations, although the nature of this list, i.e. whether it should be a list of "proscribed" or of "special facilities" destinations will require further reflexion';
- 'common criteria for the issuing of licences for exports from the EC';

- 'a forum or mechanism in which to coordinate licensing and enforcement policies and procedures';
- administrative cooperation.

The Council of Ministers set up an Ad Hoc High Level Working Party to examine the issue and in August 1992 the Commission made a formal proposal for an EC-wide regulation system.[36]

Negotiation of the dual-use regulation proved to be a protracted affair. Among many issues of concern was whether the regulation should adopt the CoCom consultative model, or whether some central licensing body should be created. Member states examined in microscopic detail the various legal, timetable and voting questions raised by the proposed regulation. One concern was whether licences issued by one member state would be valid throughout the Community, or whether member states should have a *droit de regard* over exports from their ports under licences issued by another member state. Some members called for a catch-all clause, and others for a 'safeguard' clause which could operate when national security was considered to be at stake, even in the case of exports to other EC states. Reflecting deep misgivings about the integrity of the boundary between Community competence and national prerogative, the most difficult issue was the content and purpose of the lists which would support the regulation. Some members argued that lists of sensitive technologies, of favoured or proscribed destinations and of guidelines for making export decisions came too close to foreign and security policy-making to be placed under Community competence and could not therefore form part of a Commission-based regulation system. In late 1992 the Commission accepted that these three key lists should be a matter for governments.

The issue then became one of deciding how to draw up and implement the lists, in such a way that national sensitivities could be respected. While the regulation drew its authority from Article 113 of the EEC Treaty and was therefore a matter for qualified majority voting (QMV), several governments argued that QMV would not be an appropriate way to draw up and implement the lists, given their foreign and security policy implications. Late in 1993 the Belgian government offered a compromise which was subsequently adopted. The compromise was to seek agreement on the content of the lists through the 'joint action' process of the CFSP pillar of the TEU, and to publish the lists as annexures to an intergovernmental CFSP decision rather than include them in the Commission regulation. Use of the joint-action process, which is examined more closely in Chapter 5, broke the deadlock and on 14 June 1994 ten of the then twelve Council members agreed to the adoption of the regulation. Danish and Belgian reservations were waived in the following weeks, but it was not until late December 1994 that final agreement was reached on the form and content of both the regulation[37] and the joint-action decision.[38] By now the proposed implementation date of 1 January 1995 had slipped to 1 March 1995. However, translation and administrative difficulties delayed the formal publication and implementation of the regulation, and the 1 March 1995 deadline was also postponed. This caused a certain amount of inconvenience for those governments and industries which had prepared the legal and administrative ground for the regulation and had, at the last minute, to revert to old practices. Finally, on 1 July 1995, almost three years after the Commission's original proposal, the regulation and the joint action both came into force, creating a 'Community regime for the control of exports of dual-use goods' and constituting 'an integrated system involving, in accordance with their own powers, the Council, the Commission and the Member states'.[39]

The basic aim of the regulation is to ensure that the export from 'the customs territory of the Community' of certain dual-use goods (listed in Annex I to the joint-action decision) does not take place without authorization. Intra-EU trade in these goods and in other unlisted dual-use goods is not covered by the regulation, although there is scope for governments to impose licensing requirements on such trade in certain circumstances. A central element of the regulation is the catch-all clause, a feature which aroused some controversy during negotiations. Article 4 states that the export even of unlisted goods must be licensed if the exporter is informed by his national authorities, or is simply 'aware', that the goods are intended for use in WMD or missile manufacture. It is left to member governments to decide how – or whether – to legislate in the potentially controversial matter of establishing an exporter's knowledge, or mere 'grounds for suspecting', that a given export is intended to be misused. Article 5, the 'safeguard clause', allows governments to prohibit the export of any other, unlisted dual-use goods, provided any prohibitions are notified to the Commission and other governments. Article 6 lays down the requirement to license any export of goods subject to the regulation, unless 'simplified formalities' are to be used, for example when the recipient is one of the countries listed in Annex II to the joint-action decision. Once issued, however, any individual, general or global authorization is to be valid throughout the EU. Article 7 states that export authorization is a matter for 'the competent authorities of the [member state] in which the exporter is established'. But if the goods to be exported are located elsewhere in the EU, the relevant government is granted a brief period in which to object to the export. Indeed, a member state may object to any export from the EU if it perceives its 'national interests' to be at stake, but in these cases the licensing government is required merely to 'immediately engage in consultations of a non-binding nature' with the government raising the objection. Article 8 requires member states to 'take into consideration' the 'common guidelines' annexed to the joint-action decision when deciding upon an export authorization. Article 10 permits each member state temporarily to inter-rupt the export of goods from its territory, even though the export has been licensed elsewhere in the EU, if there are grounds to suspect that the licence was issued incorrectly, or if circumstances have changed. In 'exceptional circumstances', otherwise entirely valid and proper exports can be prevented if a member state decides that the export 'would be contrary to its essential foreign policy or security interests or to the fulfilment of its international obligations or commitments'. As far as penalties are concerned, Article 17 leaves enforcement and punishment to national authorities, merely calling for any penalties to be 'effective, proportionate and dissuasive'. Remaining articles deal with administra-tive and record-keeping matters, coordination between the member states, legal arrangements and procedures to cover a 'transitional period', the duration of which is left unclear. Article 22 states, *inter alia*, that the regulation does not affect 'the application of Article 223 of the Treaty establishing the European Community'.

The joint-action decision is, by comparison, a concise and straight-forward document, the object of which is to introduce the five lists referred to in the regulation. Annex I to the joint action lists licensable dual-use equipment in ten categories:

- nuclear materials, facilities and equipment;
- materials, chemicals, 'microorganisms' and 'toxins';
- materials processing;
- electronics;
- computers;
- telecommunications and 'information security';
- sensors and lasers;
- navigation and avionics;
- marine;
- propulsion systems, space systems and related equipment.

The export outside the EU of goods in these categories is to be specifically authorized, unless the destination appears in Annex II to the joint action, a list of destinations for which 'simplified formalities may be applicable'. With Austria, Finland and Sweden having now joined the EU, Annex II lists no more than six countries: Australia, Canada, Japan, Norway, Switzerland and the United States. The omission of a list of sensitive or proscribed destinations could prove to be a grave weakness in the overall regulation, by giving governments 'significant discretion in deciding whether the proliferation risk associated with a prospective recipient country is outweighed by the benefits of exporting controlled items to that country. Such discretion could limit the effectiveness of an agreement among EU Member States on a common list of controlled goods and technologies.'[40] Annex III to the joint action lists the 'factors' which authorities will 'take into account' when deciding whether export applications should be authorized. These include commitments to international non-proliferation agreements, internationally agreed embargoes, 'considerations of national foreign and security policy' including the Luxembourg and Lisbon conventional arms export criteria, and finally, 'considerations about intended end-use and the risk of diversion'. Annex IV lists goods such as nuclear reprocessing plants, stealth technology and rocket-propulsion systems which, although already listed in Annex I, are considered by some member states to be so sensitive that for the duration of the 'transitional period', all intra-EU exports will require national authorization. Annex V lists those goods which some member states continue to define as military, rather than dual-use, and which are therefore excluded from the regulation under Article 223. Annexes III and IV, it would seem, provide a counterweight to the Commission's earlier insistence that Article 223 should be applied restrictively.

There remains, clearly, a great deal of national discretion with regard to the application of the dual-use regulation. Given that some member states are very sensitive to perceived challenges to national prerogative in the key areas of foreign policy, security and defence, a careful compromise of this sort was perhaps inevitable. In such circumstances, the combination of the Article 113/QMV regulation with a set of CFSP/unanimous lists is a notable achievement, but it remains to be seen whether the 'linked system' will be a simple and successful formula or a hopeless attempt to juxtapose two very different approaches to European cooperation.

Chapter 4

Industry

Introduction

The term 'European defence industry' is a useful shorthand expression for the purposes of this study, but may suggest more homogeneity than actually exists. Within the EU there are many national defence sectors, organized and oriented according to different national preferences and industrial practices. There is a vast array of prime and sub-contractors, and a complex set of intra- and extra-European cooperative ventures. Some sectors of defence industry have weathered the end of the Cold War better than others, but all are in a state of flux, and are experiencing or anticipating major structural change. Several different political and industrial strategies are being considered. It is nevertheless possible to identify the main arguments surrounding the future of European defence industry, and the main industrial and political challenges being faced, and on this basis to discuss the potential of the EU as a multilateral arms and technology export regulatory forum.

The various national defence sectors have three general features in common. The first is that defence industry and government are in a close relationship. This results in part from a 'national security' mentality which sees defence industry as a vital national resource, a strategic asset rather like standing armed forces. Another explanation is that governments are the sole or main customer for the products of Europe's defence industries. But if the relationship is generally close, it is not uniform. Britain, for example, has traditionally adopted a *laissez-faire* approach to defence industry and declared against adopting an interventionist defence industrial policy. The French government, on the other hand, has historically had a much closer relationship with French defence industry, as owner, manager and customer. But at both extremes the industry/

government relationship is changing. During 1995 the British government moved in the direction of a 'defence technology strategy', with talk of the need for a 'much improved relationship' between government and industry,[1] and away from the 'rigid competitive policy' of the late 1980s.[2] At roughly the same time, the French government began to warn French defence industry that the comfortable and dependable relationship of the past was coming to an end.[3] Even so, the relationship between government and defence industry in Europe generally is likely to remain very close. In these circumstances any restructuring of national defence sectors will be highly charged politically. And at the regional level, any plan or policy for the future of Europe's defence industries must satisfy, perhaps more than any other industrial sector, deeply held national commercial and political preferences. The result is likely to be political and economic distortions in the European defence sector as a whole; where the 'final customers' are solely or mainly governments, 'the problems of eliminating scope for preferential deals are especially difficult'.[4]

The second feature occurs with rather more consistency. Defence industries in Europe have a manufacturing capacity far in excess of what their customers might require, nationally or regionally. Following the end of the Cold War, domestic defence equipment markets have contracted dramatically. Table 4.1 illustrates the reduction in defence expenditure, both in real terms and as a percentage of GDP, among the current members of the EU between 1985 and 1993.

In total, the current members of the EU spent US$15,764 million (constant 1993) less on defence in 1993 than in 1985 – a reduction of 8.2 per cent. Yet, although the economic environment in which European defence industry operates has clearly become harsher over the past decade, there remains an excess in manufacturing capacity over conceivable European demand. The problem can be illustrated by main battle tank (MBT) manufacturing. By the end of 1994 the current fifteen members of the EU owned a total of about 12,500 MBTs, of various types and vintages. As all fifteen governments look to reduce their defence spending, and with Cold War armoured-warfare scenarios slipping out of fashion, the demand for new MBTs is sure to fall. Even if all European MBT manufacturers had full and equal access to this dwindling market, the competition for any remaining orders would be stiff among the three manufacturers struggling to survive: one in Britain, one in Germany and one in France. Similar duplication of resources can be found in many other European defence equipment sectors, such as warships and combat aircraft. Furthermore, with no clear sense of the level at

Table 4.1 Defence expenditure, 1985–93

	$m (constant 1993)		%GDP	
	1985	1993	1985	1993
Austria	1,696	1,650	1.2	0.9
Belgium	5,409	3,805	3.0	1.8
Denmark	2,747	2,701	2.2	2.0
Finland	1,974	2,100	2.8	2.0
France	42,918	42,898	4.0	3.4
Germany	46,330	36,654	3.2	2.1
Greece	3,060	4,074	7.0	5.5
Ireland	420	560	1.8	1.1
Italy	22,576	24,400	2.3	2.0
Luxembourg	84	117	0.9	1.0
Netherlands	7,814	7,070	3.1	2.2
Portugal	1,610	2,360	3.1	2.8
Spain	9,900	7,870	2.4	1.5
Sweden	4,194	5,500	3.3	2.3
UK	41,891	35,100	5.2	3.6

Source: 'International comparison of defence expenditure and military manpower in 1985, 1992 and 1993', tables prepared for but not printed in *The Military Balance 1994–95* (London: IISS, 1994).

which defence spending will 'bottom out', surplus manufacturing capability could prove to be a permanent feature; 'continuous disarmament creates permanent overcapacity'.[5] The problem of overcapacity is compounded by the fact that defence industry continues to be viewed predominantly through a national prism. The result is that manufacturing overcapacities do not automatically translate into market-led restructuring of the overall European supply base, as they might in a more straightforward market. And for as long as governments resist the discipline of a Europe-wide market for the sake of national protectionism, distortions in Europe's defence industrial base will persist and will make the overall reduction and rationalization of manufacturing capacity slow and difficult.

The situation in Europe stands in marked contrast to that in the United States, and this introduces the final general feature of European defence industry: the fact of extra-European competition, mainly but not exclusively from the United States. A useful, simple comparator is the market for MBTs. With a 1994 stockpile of some 15,000 MBTs, the size of the MBT market in the United States is not very much greater than that in the EU. More significant is the fact that the United States has one defence market, rather than fifteen, and one defence budget which, in 1993, stood at over US$297 billion; more than $1 billion greater than the defence budgets of all current EU members combined. The United States also has one defence policy, one style of government-industry dealings and, above all, one MBT manufacturer. The US defence industry is able to achieve standards of efficiency and economies of scale that European manufacturers cannot at present match. With higher production costs and lower production volumes, European defence manufacturers face stiff competition for any international export orders.[6] To make matters worse, the price and quality of US defence equipment often undermines attempts to pursue a 'buy European' policy, as the Dutch and British decisions in 1995 to buy the McDonnell Douglas AH-64 *Apache* attack helicopter illustrate.

Restructuring the market

In the face of straitening national defence budgets and inadequate national procurement shopping lists, one response is to seek to broaden the scope of the market in which Europe's defence industries sell their products. Market expansion could occur in three ways. First, Europe's manufacturers could be given open access to the whole of a European defence equipment market. Open access would have to be awarded equally, across the EU. But since there are known to be overcapacities in all defence manufacturing sectors, even when the maximum size of any Europe-wide market is taken into account, it would seem that open access could only be efficient and ensure the survival of some manufacturers in certain member states, if it were accepted that other manufacturers, in other member states, would face closure. The underlying sources of national defence industrial protectionism would therefore have to be addressed at some point, and it seems unlikely that these issues could be resolved as a happy consequence of an open EU defence market. A second option might be described as the 'transatlantic' solution. The idea that NATO's defence manufacturers should all have equal access to defence equipment markets on both sides of the Atlantic has received a good deal of attention, both during and after the Cold War. In 1989 and 1990 some impetus was given to the creation of a 'two-way street' in transatlantic defence trade. But subsequent attempts to create a more productive atmosphere, such as the efforts of NATO's Conference of National Armaments Directors to agree a politically binding 'Code of Conduct' for intra-alliance defence trade, were described in late 1994 as developing 'slowly' and 'cantankerously'.[7] The politics of the pork barrel operate on both sides of the Atlantic. And even if enlightened self-interest did prevail, and a genuinely open transatlantic market did come about, Europe's defence manufacturers would still have to compete against US giants, such as Lockheed Martin, producing high-quality, well-priced and often battle-proven equipment.

The third and final market-expansion option sees Europe's defence manufacturers venturing into the international export market and fighting for a global market share. The export option is attractive, and a standard response to defence industrial overcapacity.[8] European defence industries would undoubtedly offer keen competition in many areas. But at a time of global recession in defence spending, resulting in a contracting global defence market, Europe's industries face extremely stiff competition for export orders. Competition comes not only from US manufacturers but also from 'second tier' producers, particularly those in Southeast Asia and the Asia-Pacific region. And the long-awaited Russian arms export drive might also intrude upon the scene.

The reality is that attempts to modify and broaden the market for European defence equipment do not in themselves offer a solution to manufacturing overcapacity in Europe. The problem is not simply one of market access and vigorous marketing. The three options discussed above all point in one direction: restructuring of the manufacturing side. Market expansion has to take place, but 'streamlining of what is left of the European defence industrial base takes precedence'.[9] Only then will it be possible for overcapacities to be reduced and for European industry to compete on something approaching an equal footing with its US counterparts.

Restructuring the manufacturers

The key questions now become how and where might such restructuring take place, and when; and what might the effect be upon efforts to establish in the EU a multilateral regulatory system? Since the 1980s European defence industry has tried to follow two, not obviously compatible, paths to restructuring.[10] The first path involves consolidation at the national level, and the creation of monopoly suppliers. The second path amounts to the 'Europeanization' and 'internationalization' of the European defence industry through the development of transnational ties. The second path presents two broad possibilities, one of which is the 'project-led' restructuring of the sort currently favoured by the British government. As far as the British government is concerned, project-led restructuring is defined more by the dynamics of the market than the politics of European integration. The second transnational restructuring option would involve a European defence industrial 'big bang', with full-scale reorganization and rationalization of the region's defence industries. This option can barely be examined or understood outside the context of European political integration and will accordingly be defined here as 'supranational restructuring'.

National restructuring

Restructuring or concentration at the national level reflects the determination to sustain national self-sufficiency in defence manufacturing. In order to mitigate the effect of manufacturing surpluses and other inefficiencies, government and industry might embark upon a policy of 'vertical integration', whereby certain manufacturers would receive special status in government procurement competitions, enabling the company to absorb its national competitors and persuading it to specialize in that manufacturing area. This 'national-champion' approach could result in one or very few national defence giants providing all manufacturing and prime contractor services for government. Although the general trend is for national consolidation to be sought in parallel with internationalization, some supporters of the national-champion approach reject the latter idea; the chairman of Britain's GEC has described the idea of 'cross-border rationalisation in the European defence industry as naive, since all main European countries will ... want to maintain a strong element of self-sufficiency'.[11] Some Swedish industrialists apparently share similar views, as do some in France. In spite of changes in the government-industry relationship in France, the national-champion approach remains popular in French industry and government, where it is also viewed as a possible basis for supranational restructuring.

There are several questions to be asked about the national-champion approach, not least whether governments as customers could any longer receive the benefits and value for money which they would expect in a more openly competitive environment. It is also difficult to accept that any national defence budget alone could sustain one or a small number of such national champions, however well restructured and efficient they may be. And if the post-Cold War requirement for military equipment is unable to match the political determination to sustain a national defence industrial base, the result might be that governments are forced to prop up uncompetitive industries with increased subsidies. Defence companies protected in such a way would certainly be able to produce good defence equipment, but might find it more difficult to produce equipment of the highest quality within a reasonable budget. Foreign customers might therefore prove hard to come by, especially as the global 'buyer's market' continues to contract. But whatever the difficulties, government and industry would simply have to expand foreign sales. Not only would governments in this position be tempted to assist industry through export credit guarantees and further subsidies, they would also be unlikely to accept any collective export regulation system which might restrain sales. Of all the options available, the 'national-champion' approach is therefore least compatible with the development of an effective EU export control regime.

Project-led restructuring
Between national consolidation and supranational restructuring lies the 'project-led' option, championed by the British government and popular with industry. The project-led approach seeks to satisfy two demands: the economic and political imperatives of European defence industrial consolidation on one hand, and commercial competitiveness on the other. Governments and industry have already developed a range of cooperative and collaborative arrangements: project consortia such as the Anglo-French-Italian 'Project Horizon' air-defence frigate programme, joint-stock venture companies such as the 1993 initiative between GEC-Marconi (UK) and Thomson-CSF (France) to study the feasibility of new radar equipment, equity swaps, cross-border mergers and acquisitions and co-marketing agreements. Where the project-led approach departs from past practice is in its rejection of IEPG-style work-sharing arrangements known as *juste retour*, whereby collaborative projects were divided proportionately between participating countries, often with little account taken of the skill and efficiency of the various national defence sectors. *Juste retour* was a political response to the need for defence industrial collaboration, but fostered national and Europe-wide inefficiencies. In the name of competitiveness, the project-led approach rejects both *juste retour* and the 'Euro-champion' idea discussed below.

The main argument against project-led consolidation is that European defence industry can be both collaborative and competitive, and therefore efficient, only to the extent that the whole edifice is held together with the glue of political commitment to European integration in areas of high politics. Yet Britain's adherence to competitive defence procurement has so far prevented such a leap of faith. While calling for greater efficiency in Europe's defence industrial base, Britain has nevertheless repeatedly rejected calls for European preference and often bought US equipment 'off the shelf'. The interim purchase of C-130J transport aircraft and the AH-64 attack-helicopter contract are but two examples of a practice which has exasperated integration-minded defence industrialists and politicians throughout Europe. Many of Europe's defence industrialists view competition with their US counterparts as inherently unfair. By this view, British procurement of US equipment not only impedes the essential process of integration in Europe, it also makes it easier for US government and industry to sabotage the consolidation of European defence industry and thereby retain competitive advantage.[12] At the *Eurosatory '94* defence exhibition in June 1994, eleven European defence manufacturing associations signed an agreement which 'essentially circled the wagons against the United States' by calling for 'an internal defense market to ensure that European equipment is competitive', and for 'buy European' procurement policies in Europe.[13]

Supranational restructuring

Supranational restructuring involves a combination of vertical and horizontal integration, and is the most highly charged option politically. The basic principle is that Europe's defence equipment requirements would be provided by 'Euro-champions': defence industrial 'clusters' offering one MBT manufacturer, one combat-aircraft manufacturer, one warship manufacturer, and so forth. These clusters would be big, and fit enough to compete on the world stage.[14] Euro-champions could be organized in one of two ways. Assuming that EC anti-trust legislation and commercial policies could be waived or ignored, in each manufacturing sector transnational monopolies could be allowed to consolidate. Alternatively, each sector could be served by national specialists: Germany as Europe's MBT manufacturer, Britain for warships and France for combat aircraft, for example. France and Italy are among EU members which have expressed an interest in such an approach, and some European defence industrialists have taken a similar position.[15]

A division of labour along the lines of a 'defence industrial Yalta' is, however, unlikely without a wholly new political climate in Europe; 'such a scenario implies a willingness to give up a wide range of capabilities and to accept dependence on others'.[16] Even if the political climate were to become more suitable, there would still be difficult decisions to make as to the allocation of specializations and the sharing of benefits;

responsibility for Europe's MBTs would be considered less generally beneficial for a national economic and industrial base than responsibility for combat-aircraft manufacturing. And there would still have to be some means of ensuring that the overall system remained internally competitive, with national governments receiving value for money.

Implications for export regulation

Deeply entrenched ideological positions, and the apparent willingness in some quarters to accept inefficiency and overcapacity as the inevitable costs of national defence industrial protectionism, suggest that any restructuring will be slow, if progress is made at all.[17] Whatever the outcome, defence exports are sure to have a central role in any national, project-led or supranational approach to restructuring. It was suggested earlier that national consolidation alone would have the most destructive effect on attempts to create an EU-wide export regulatory system. For the most part, however, national consolidation is seen as a complement, rather than an alternative, to some form of international cooperation.[18] The most immediate difficulty with the project-led approach is the problem of ownership of the transnational venture, and the question of responsibility for compliance with export control guidelines.

Ownership and responsibility

If the 'market-led' restructuring option continues to be pursued, with more cross-border joint-venture companies and project consortia being established, questions arise as to the ownership and legal status of such industrial bodies; who – or what – is responsible to whom for compliance with export controls and guidelines? At what level of political authority should such controls and guidelines be issued? Transatlantic and global collaborative ventures could also present similar problems, as could Euro-champion transnational conglomerates. Could such bodies make it possible to avoid national and multilateral export policies and restrictions? Or could they simply make the task of export control, nationally and regionally, more difficult than it would otherwise be? Since defence consolidation is in part driven by the desire to compete more vigorously and effectively in what remains of the European and world defence markets, attempts to regulate trade in weapons and technology might be unwelcome. There is already some evidence to suggest that the export of multinationally produced defence equipment causes difficulty for national and multilateral export control systems, even for relatively anodyne international initiatives such as the United Nations Register of Conventional Arms.

There could be basic inconsistencies between an export control system which operates as a collective effort by fifteen governments, and a pattern of defence consolidation which produces new, cross-border industrial and political entities. By one account, governmental influence upon European defence industry is already diminishing, with defence companies 'following the directives of the authorities less and less'.[19] But other analysts argue that large multinational defence companies are not inherently more difficult to control than smaller companies. After all, every trading company has to be registered somewhere, and when it does so it comes under a national jurisdiction. Larger firms may, in addition, be more anxious to understand and comply with all relevant export control regulations, simply because they have more to lose in the event of misunderstandings or wilful non-compliance.[20] Most legitimate exporters of weapons and sensitive technology appear to accept that the international defence market is not a free-for-all and that exports should conform to national practices and to nationally implemented multilateral agreements. In any case, the gradual assumption of extra-territorial powers by European governments should tighten the regulatory grip.

If the various modes of project-led transnational consolidation cause difficulties, these should not be overstated. Provided sufficient regulation can be achieved at some level, project-led consolidation does not present a *prima facie* case for an export control authority at a commensurate – i.e. supranational – level in Europe. This may be a complacent view, too accepting of a situation which is, arguably, commercially inefficient and unstable. But it is a view which corresponds to the current parameters of the defence industrial consolidation debate. The question is, can these parameters, and the possibilities and expectations which follow, be altered? Is the project-led approach merely the least bad course while the political commitment to trans-European defence industrial consolidation is lacking? Any regulatory challenges posed by project-led, *ad hoc* consolidation clearly have to be addressed. But a more serious, structural problem may be that governments' unwillingness to make concessions to collective organization and discipline in these areas of high politics will always prevent the development of common export policies and practices. Furthermore, without a common regulatory framework, industry may be prevented from achieving the standards of efficiency and competitiveness which are required, never aspiring to anything more than *ad hoc* project-led arrangements; one prominent German defence industrialist has called for 'common rules and guidelines for exports' as a necessary precondition for a 'truly European arms industry'.[21] Questions of 'political restructuring' form a persistent sub-text to the defence industrial consolidation debate, and cannot for long be excluded from the discussion.

Political restructuring

Any discussion of trans- or supranational authority in the defence field soon turns to Article 223 of the EEC Treaty, frequently cited as the main stumbling block to Commission regulation of an ill-organized and inefficient European defence sector. By one view, Article 223 is an anomaly which 'hinders the market-driven restructuring that government and industry leaders say is vital for European defence contractors to compete in the international market. And as long as Article 223 remains in force, governments will find it difficult to resist the urge to micromanage industry's restructuring.'[22] It could equally be argued that Article 223 enables governments to avoid altogether the difficult task of restructuring.

As with the question of industrial ownership, it is possible to over-state, or at least misconstrue, the problem of Article 223. Too often, Article 223 is described as if it were an external imposition, a foreign body the simple excision of which would make way for harmonious and efficient industrial restructuring. Of course, if Article 223 were to be deleted by the 1996 IGC, or at some subsequent time, the effect on multilateral export controls in the EU would be dramatic. National and cross-border mergers and acquisitions would all have to run the gauntlet of EC competition policy. National subsidies such as export credit guarantees could all be challenged. Elaborate compromises between Community competence and national prerogative, as in the dual-use regulation, would no longer be necessary. Defence-related exports would, arguably, be as much a matter for EC competence as for the CFSP pillar of the EU, and a fully centralized decision-making authority for the regulation of defence exports could result. But Article 223 is a home-grown political device, and its excision is likely to be much less neat. What is at issue is not merely a clause in a treaty, but fundamental concerns over the scope and direction of political integration in the EU. There are signs, even in France, that governments are increasingly willing to relax their special interest in defence industry and accept some form of cross-border industrial rationalization. All this suggests that uncompromising protectionism, of which Article 223 is a symbol, is considered by governments to be less suitable and realistic for post-Cold War Europe. This is not, of course, tantamount to saying that national preference has been or will be abandoned altogether. But if the pattern of change in the politico-industrial relationship is a matter of evolution rather than revolution, it could be that the precise requirements for common export licensing and regulation will only be revealed gradually. These functions could of course be served by the Commission, but this would require a more abrupt departure from past practice than governments seem able or willing to contemplate at present. Alternatively, if major changes in the political make-up of the EU are unlikely in the short term, it could be more productive to ask how far governments are willing to 'pool' their authority and what sort of intergovernmental organization they would be willing to accept, rather than remain trapped in the rhetoric surrounding Article 223.

The main difficulty is that there is a logic to European defence industrial rationalization which outstrips the pace at which political integration is taking place in the sensitive areas of foreign, security and defence policies. It can persuasively be argued that one part of the solution to the EU's arms manufacturing overcapacity is to allow defence firms to compete freely, across the EU, in a 'European Defence Equipment Market' (EDEM). An EDEM, like its commercial cousin, would require some form of organization and regulation, and a legal framework. Given that the manufacture and purchase of defence equipment is driven by the requirements of a small number of governments, it is clear that the organization running an EDEM would be no more or less than an EU common procurement agency. Regulation of defence procurement caught the eye of the Commission some time ago,[23] and the Commission 'has gradually increased its authority in the defence industry field, by adopting a position on joint ventures and on acquisitions in the defence industry that have been based on the existing paragraphs on competition policy in the Treaty of Rome'.[24] But the Commission's authority over activities in the defence sector is heavily circumscribed, as is suggested by the British decision in October 1994 to cite 'essential security interests' and invoke Article 223 in order to exclude the Commission from involvement in the British Aerospace bid for Vickers Shipbuilding and Engineering Ltd.[25] The more established route to cooperation in defence procurement has, instead, so far been intergovernmental. The WEU Declaration published with the Maastricht Treaty called for 'enhanced cooperation in the field of armaments with the aim of creating a European armaments agency'.[26] The WEU duly set up a new agency: the Western European Armaments Group (WEAG). In December 1992 the WEAG took over from the IEPG, and set its sights on the creation of a European defence procurement system of the sort which the IEPG had called for in its December 1990 Copenhagen document.

At some point, however, a relatively straightforward question must be asked: on behalf of whom, or what, would a common procurement agency act? If the motive is simply efficiency and the avoidance of waste, something like the British 'project-led' model of restructuring could apply. When EU governments identify a common need for, say, a combat aircraft or warship, it would make sense to manage the competition among competing consortia and perhaps then, on behalf of the customer-governments, manage relations with prime contractors up to the point at which the equipment is delivered. But for others, viewing defence procurement and industrial restructuring as an element of European political integration, the attraction of a common procurement agency is that it may lead to a common European defence system. There is, however, some uncertainty about the ordering of the relationship between common procurement and common defence. A survey of European national armaments directors in June 1994 found that some EU members such as the Netherlands saw that highly integrated procurement policies could promote a common defence policy. Other EU members, however, saw a common defence policy as the necessary precursor.[27]

The difference in approaches can be seen most readily in contrasting views of the role and expansion of the bilateral Franco-German armaments agency. The agency was created in December 1993, to be responsible for joint procurement and research and development, and to assist in the creation of the Franco-German 'Eurocorps'. From the outset there were fears that the bilateral body would challenge and undermine the agency called for in the 1991 WEU Declaration, just as there were fears that the 'Eurocorps' itself would undermine the European 'pillar' of NATO. Partly to allay these concerns, during 1994 the French and German governments allowed their agency to move closer to the WEU. By the end of the same year the WEU had postponed its own plans to establish a European armaments agency. But the goal of a European armaments agency was not abandoned altogether; with no rival, the Franco-German body was increasingly seen as a nucleus of the wider organization.[28] In late 1994 and 1995, with more WEAG members applying for membership of the expanding Franco-German body, the two founders saw their idea being overcome by the political wrangling which had already bedevilled the WEU's efforts in this field. Disagreements developed over the purpose and future of the agency. Britain, willing to join the club only if the rules could first be changed to its satisfaction, argued for no more than a 'joint projects office' and appeared, particularly to France, to be obstructing attempts to turn common procurement into deeper political and strategic cooperation. Disagreement also grew over whether a commitment to European preference was a reasonable condition for membership of the agency.

Discussion of the relationship between common procurement and common defence is unavoidably circular; it is not yet clear whether an EU procurement system will be the cause or the consequence of political integration in defence and security policies. It is not even clear that common procurement, however it comes about, will be the best solution industrially and commercially: 'The risk exists that joint procurement – which may be years away – could end up just coddling local arms makers.'[29] But what can be said is that before the process can go much further, a degree of political commitment will have to be made. If one object of common EU procurement is to supply standard equipment made by European defence firms to European forces, then there must at some point be agreement to create those forces, agree their missions, and agree their operational military requirements. Without such agreements, any EU system of defence procurement, and defence restructuring as a whole, will lack a vital rationale. Similar things might be said of calls for a common export control agency. Defence industrial restructuring in Europe is aimed not only at the European market, but also at international exports. If an EDEM would create the need for some form of EU procurement agency, so activity in the export market by 'Euro-industries' would require management by a common export agency. Once again, defence industry appears broadly in favour of such an agency,[30] although industry's concern is more to clarify and harmonize EU export arrangements, and make them more efficient, than to contribute to the debate over political integration.[31] In the end, however, the political dimension cannot be avoided. No discussion of defence industrial restructuring, defence procurement, arms export policies and Article 223 can continue for long before the questions of common foreign, security and defence policies arise. Before examining these issues in Chapter 5, the present chapter turns finally to the internationalization of defence manufacturing and global technology transfer.

Internationalization of defence industry

The pursuit of foreign partners and subsidiaries is not unique to Europe's defence industries. It is normal practice for all firms, not just those in the defence sector, to seek foreign connections in order to share costs and reduce risks, gain access to foreign innovation, achieve economies of scale and penetrate foreign markets. When domestic economic conditions are unfavourable and risks are at their highest, pressure to seek international partners can be strong. Accordingly, internationalization has become especially popular with Europe's defence sector.[32] Joint ventures and international mergers can be global as well as European. In some cases, defence companies have been tempted to shift whole sectors of their production cycle to developing regions in order to take advantage of cheaper labour and production costs and unrivalled expertise in the manufacture of certain key sub-components such as semi-conductors. This process, known as 'off-shoring', has been especially noticeable in the 1990s. Often, the chosen site has been the Asia-Pacific region and Southeast Asia, with Taiwan, Indonesia, South Korea and Singapore being highly favoured.[33] Internationalization inevitably involves the transfer of technology and manufacturing skills. Often though, technology transfers take place in a more deliberate way, as part of offset arrangements in arms-transfer deals. As the pursuit of foreign partners and the willingness to transfer technology through offsets become increasingly important for European defence manufacturing, so the task of multilateral export control becomes more complex and difficult.

The spread of arms manufacturing capability

Internationalization of defence industry inevitably leads to the diffusion of weapons-related manufacturing capability. In most cases, unavoidably export-oriented European defence industries do not have the luxury of choice; in exchange for market access most clients now demand the transfer of manufacturing technology in the form of direct technology transfers, sub-contracting deals, and licensed co-development and co-production. Although most production still takes place among the traditional 'first tier' of weapons suppliers, the result of internationalization is that a significant 'second tier' as well as a less important 'third tier' of weapon producers have now developed.[34] Often, states appear keen to acquire an arms manufacturing capability in the face of the harshest commercial and economic logic. This points to an important feature of the spread of arms manufacturing capabilities around the world; the spread is the result both of supplier industry 'push' and recipient 'pull'. The 'indigenization' of weapons production capability is partly a result of arms manufacturing being seen as an attribute of a sovereign and politically mature state. Rather than attempt to build up an arms industry from nothing, a goal which would require decades of industrial and scientific development to be condensed into a few years, most states take advantage of offset agreements made in connection with arms purchases in order to ensure the acquisition of the necessary technology and skills.[35] Offsets commonly involve an agreement by the supplier to co-produce the weapon or its parts with the recipient country and, in time, even to license full production. Given the decline in domestic markets and the creation of a more open, worldwide 'buyer's market' for arms, offset demands are becoming increasingly difficult to resist. A good example of the spread of technology through offset deals is the South Korean purchase of General Dynamics F-16 fighters from the United States. Korea will purchase 12 planes direct, assemble 36 from production kits prepared in Fort Worth, and make the remaining 72 in Samsung Industries in Seoul.[36] But perhaps the best known are the arrangements made between Saudi Arabia and various arms and technology suppliers. In the 1980s Saudi Arabia signed deals with the United States, Britain and France which involved the transfer of technology and know-how. The 'primary goal' of Saudi Arabia's offset programme was described as 'self-sufficiency in the high technology civil and, where feasible, defence industrial sectors'.[37]

Self-sufficiency in arms manufacturing results not only from permissiveness in the transfer of technology through offsets, however. Perversely, inconsistent policies or over-zealous export controls and embargoes can have a similar effect. Israel's response to the fickle behaviour of suppliers was both to seek a variety of suppliers, in order to reduce dependence on any single one, and, from the mid-1950s, to develop its own defence sector. Israel never achieved self-sufficiency in its arms industry, but certainly became a considerable exporter during the 1980s. SIPRI ranked Israel as the twelfth largest arms exporter for the period 1981–90, and according to Israel's own estimates, arms and equipment worth some US$1,500 million were exported in 1989.[38] Defence industrial self-sufficiency was, however, achieved by South Africa. The November 1977 UN embargo banned the supply of defence equipment to South Africa and prevented UN members buying South African weapons. According to one assessment, 'The arms embargo ... obliged South Africa's defence industry to become largely self-sufficient in providing military equipment for the [South African Defence Force] ... By the late 1980s the domestic defence industry had acquired across-the-board production capabilities and was able to supply the SADF with the bulk of its equipment needs.' Clandestine measures were often used to acquire key technologies, and some firms evaded the embargo by using South African subsidiaries. South Africa's arms industry flourished and the country became a major arms exporter in its own right, especially to fellow 'pariah' states and regimes.[39] South Africa never had much respect for the embargo,[40] but when it was lifted on 25 May 1994 the way was open to expand into the world arms market.

The internationalization of conventional weapons production, and the arrival on the scene of a number of small but perfectly formed arms and technology suppliers, able to dominate niches in the international market and to supply to 'renegade regimes',[41] suggest that the management of the international arms trade may now have moved well beyond the control of any relatively small group of supplier governments, even where those governments agree to act completely in concert. When fully coordinated, supplier cartels might be able to manage their own sector of the international market but probably ought not to expect to manage the market as a whole. The difficulty is that, once this limitation is perceived, it feeds back to and undermines the very notion of limited supply-side coordination. In these circumstances, the best that might be expected is some form of 'transparency' confidence-building measure, of the sort offered by the UN Conventional Arms Register, if and when it is expanded to include domestic procurement and weapons production. More ambitiously, 'leading edge' weapons manufacturers and exporters may be able to identify and restrict access to new, strategically important technologies, but this too is becoming increasingly difficult.

Diffusion of technology

The strategic impact of new military technology is a subject of endless fascination. Recent accounts often refer to film footage taken of cruise missiles 'turning left' at road junctions in Baghdad during the 1991 bombardment, and precision-guided munitions disappearing down ventilation shafts; there can be no doubt that the technological sophistication of modern weaponry is increasing at a rapid rate. Among the projects currently running in western defence research laboratories, the possible development of micro-robot 'soldier ants' is particularly striking.[42] The thirst for sophisticated military equipment is spreading around the world; Malaysia, for example, is reportedly determined to produce its own precision-guided 'smart' munitions.[43] Advocates of the so-called 'Revolution in Military Affairs' see the current phase of military innovation as heralding a new era in military technology and strategy.[44] An alternative view is that the current 'revolution' is no more than the latest phase in a period of continuous rapid development which began in the mid-nineteenth century and which looks set to continue.[45]

The origins, duration and strategic impact of modern military technological innovation are of less interest here than the implications for attempts to control the rate and scope of technological diffusion. Are export-control policies based upon the relatively simple premise that key technology can be 'owned', and denied to outsiders, any longer possible or wise? Is it possible for the most advanced industrial nations to maintain the leading edge in military technology? The first problem which industrialized governments confront in this regard is the increasing difficulty of distinguishing between civilian and military technological development and application. The notion of 'spin-off' has been familiar since the 1950s; military research laboratories consumed vast sums for research and development and, occasionally, an application emerged which could have innocent civilian use. But during the 1970s and 1980s the 'direction of dependence' began to change and innovation began to flow from the commercial to the military sector, 'a trajectory characterized by spin-on rather than spin-off'.[46] In some cases, leading-edge civilian firms have moved 'horizontally' into the defence sector, thus adding to the pressure on already beleaguered defence industries. The civilianization of leading-edge technological development is becoming so marked that the expression 'dual-use technology' is losing the precision it may once have had and is coming to mean nothing more than 'technology' itself. In some cases, the distinction between civil and military is deliberately blurred, as in the US 'Technology Reinvestment Project' which seeks out for special funding those military research projects which can have civilian applications.[47] The US programme has led, for example, to military global positioning satellite (GPS) locating devices being used in family cars, and combat-fighter software being used in the entertainment industry.[48] Other examples of civilian use of military-related technology and equipment include image-intensifying and infra-red night-vision and surveillance devices, data compression for rapid image and information transmission, lasers, mine detection, and obstacle-avoidance alarms for helicopter pilots. British promotion of 'dual-use technology centres' emulates the US policy.[49]

The commercialization of technological innovation implies a diminution of government control over strategically significant research and development. Particularly in liberal, free-market democracies, the scope for government control of commercial research is already limited. What is more, as technological capability spreads around the world, more states are becoming highly competent on or just behind the leading edge, even to the extent of dominating important niches such as semi-conductors. The commodities being traded are also changing. There is now much more interest in trading spare parts, components and upgrade packages,[50] to the extent that the transfer of technology is becoming a more important 'medium of exchange' than completed weapons platforms.[51] As trade becomes more technology-based, as technology increasingly has both civil and military applications, and as technological diffusion occurs by 'intangible' means, or in the mind of a scientist, so the trade is becoming 'almost impossible to control'.[52] If technology denial policies are becoming difficult, there are also arguments to suggest that they are unfair. Restricted access to those 'bronze medal technologies' which have become part of 'modern industrial and silicon society' could condemn some states to 'third class industrialization and a perpetually lower standard of living'.[53] Almost thirty years ago, D.S. Landes predicted the practical and political problems which would obstruct policies of technology denial:

> The one ingredient of modernization that is just about indispensable is technological maturity and the industrialization that goes with it; otherwise one has the trappings without the substance, the pretence without the reality ... This world, which has never before been ready to universally accept any of the universal faiths offered for its salvation, is apparently prepared to embrace the religion of science and technology without reservation.[54]

For all these reasons, technology denial and export control policies face an uphill struggle. If technology denial is applied unwisely the effect could be to drive thwarted clients down the path of WMD development and deployment. One approach could be to focus upon those 'leveraging technologies' which could help to create 'military capabilities of strategic consequence',[55] but this may imply a model of deterrence, based on mutual respect for certain weapons, which may simply not be available in the conventional sphere. Furthermore, if it continues to be possible to fight wars with second- or third-rate weapons, and even with basic agricultural implements, then the obsession with leading-edge weaponry could prove dangerously misplaced. The developed world could find itself equipped more and more with 'baroque arsenals' but wholly ill-equipped to deal with low-level conflict breaking out around the world.[56] If, in spite of these reservations, technology denial and export control remain the preferred responses, there is another fundamental decision to be made. Should the focus of the denial policy be upon the 'end-use' (i.e. a commodity-list approach) or the 'end-user' (i.e. a country-list approach)? The British government has argued that the latter is the most reasonable and reliable course but, as the negotiations over the successor to CoCom have shown, others are more in favour of a 'shift away from a mind-set that focuses on lists of technology that countries deny either in general or to specific destinations', to an approach which places more emphasis on 'managing the uses to which that technology is put'.[57]

Chapter 5

Politics

Introduction

Chapters 2 and 3 have shown that, while willing to cooperate in the management of defence-related trade, some EU member governments have set strict limitations on the extent and character of any cooperation. And in Chapter 4 it became clear that defence industrial consolidation in the EU raises more than just practical difficulties and cannot be discussed as if taking place in a political vacuum. A *leitmotif* in the development of the EU has been the distinction – often more imagined than real – between the competence of central, supranational authority and that of national governments. In spite of the complex and highly integrated industrial, commercial and economic arrangements which have developed since the 1950s, dismissive expressions such as 'low politics' and 'common market' have been used to suggest a boundary, beyond which lies the 'high politics' of foreign, security and defence policies. The latter have been portrayed as the last bastion of state sovereignty and national prerogative, with member governments resisting the 'federalism' and 'creeping competence' of the supranational 'headquarters' in Brussels. Cooperation in high politics is not inconceivable, but when it has taken place the preference has generally been for intergovernmentalism, with the outcome less a single integrated policy than a compromise between various national policies. In 1996 the EU will conduct a full review of its founding document, the Maastricht Treaty on European Union. The remit of the Intergovernmental Conference is to review the Treaty and assess the implications of an expanded membership. Cooperation in foreign policy, security and defence is expected to occupy a large part of the agenda, with the detailed procedures and expectations of CFSP and the joint-action process receiving much attention. Since the manufacture, procurement and export of conventional arms and sensitive technologies all clearly have connotations of 'high policy', the planned review of cooperation in these areas is sure to have implications for the development of common export control policies. The aim of this chapter is to gauge how, or indeed whether, the political dimension of the export control debate might develop in the near term.

EU 'external policy'

If the common foreign, security and defence policies of the EU are never to be more than the cautious agreement of member governments to cooperate in certain, usually peripheral, areas without 'surrendering' national authority, then it would be unreasonable to expect the outcome to be different from similar attempts at cooperation in these policy areas by any other group of like-minded states. As for the management of defence-related trade, there would be little reason to expect the result to be any more integrated or effective than other past and current efforts at multilateral management. But this prognosis extends from a portrayal of the EU high-politics debate which is too stark. What is often obscured by the rhetoric is that the EU has become an important international actor in its own right and that, even in areas of high politics, the boundaries between national prerogative and Community competence have become difficult to define and sustain. With an 'external policy' rubric covering commercial and economic matters, the EU has been 'from its inception an international phenomenon'.[1] What is more, member governments have been willing to transfer 'most of their sovereignty in the field of foreign trade policy to the Community'.[2] For the convinced 'Euro-sceptic', pursuit of the Common Commercial Policy (CCP) and the part played by the EU as a unitary negotiator during the GATT negotiations, could all be dismissed as nothing more than the inevitable extra-EU dimensions of its low-politics functions. But even at this level, the boundary between 'high' and 'low' is often less clear than might be imagined. The dual-use regulation discussed in Chapter 3 is a good example of this overlap; the regulation itself (rather than the joint action and its annexes) is based on Article 113 of the 1958 EEC Treaty, the decision-making mechanism described as being 'central to the whole edifice' of the CCP.[3]

European political cooperation

The EU also has a more explicit tradition of cooperation in high politics. EPC sought to enable informal, *ad hoc* cooperation in certain foreign policy areas and it, too, contributed to the blurring of the boundaries between 'external' and 'foreign', 'low' and 'high'. As EPC developed during the 1970s the decision to exclude the Commission from its proceedings became untenable, particularly when foreign *economic* policy was clearly an integral part of foreign policy. The October 1981 London Report finally admitted the Commission to full association with EPC.[4] Until the 1986 Single European Act, EPC functioned outside the legal framework of the EC. Although the role of the Commission in foreign policy-making was not significantly enhanced,[5] Title III of the SEA gave EPC a basis in EC law, and attempted to bring the process closer to the objectives and procedures of the EC. Member governments were now to endeavour 'jointly to formulate and implement a European foreign policy' (SEA Article 30.1) and were to 'co-ordinate their positions more closely on the political and economic aspects of security' (SEA Art. 30.6.a). The Commission was to be 'fully associated with the proceedings' of EPC (SEA Art. 30.3.b), although the process was to remain essentially intergovernmental. This was the new mould in which member governments were able to reach agreement on a variety of arms export supervision and management matters: the list of eight criteria, the common reference list, the arms embargo framework and the comparison of national arms export administrative practices. In November 1993, with the ratification of the Treaty on European Union,[6] EPC was replaced by the CFSP. Whereas foreign policy cooperation had previously taken place in the shadow of the EC, in a relationship which, although intensifying, was still uneasy and cautious, it now became one of the three 'pillars' of the new European Union. In spite of the hope held by the Commission and some member governments that the TEU would result in a merger of EC and EPC and a fully integrated foreign and security policy-making machinery,[7] CFSP remained an intergovernmental process. The role of the Commission in foreign policy-making was enhanced, but cautiously so. The Commission's right of initiative, which it had previously enjoyed exclusively in EC-related areas, was extended into matters of foreign and security policy but was to be shared with member governments.[8] As for the European Parliament, although the TEU gave it the power to negotiate directly with the Council of Ministers, it remained largely on the periphery of any foreign policy-related activity.

By differentiating so firmly between intergovernmental and supranational policy areas or 'pillars', the TEU might well be thought to have halted rather than encouraged progress towards more integrated foreign policy-making in the EU. EPC was hardly the embodiment of a fully mature supranational foreign policy, but its semi-formal nature did suggest a certain flexibility and even dynamism, and it might have been possible to devise more imaginative and integrated procedures as time went on. Yet the TEU did advance the debate in a number of important ways, and although CFSP is best understood as an aspiration, it cannot fairly be said that CFSP is merely EPC in another, more rigid guise. In the first place, the TEU prompted the Commission to embark upon a 'bicephalous' approach to external/foreign policy. In May 1993 a new Directorate General was established (DG1A) with responsibility for external political relations. The original DG1 retained its 'traditional agenda' of 'explicitly economic issues'.[9] The new directorate faced opposition both within the Commission and from member governments as it tried to establish its role, but it was nevertheless clear that the creation of DG1A represented a further blurring of the boundaries referred to earlier, with the EU coming closer than ever before to having its own 'foreign ministry'. In October 1994 the new Commission President, Jacques Santer, reorganized the various external-relations portfolios within the Commission. For the five years from January 1995 the Commission is to be organized along more geographical than functional lines. There was, however, no suggestion of acquiescence in the Commission's outlook; in the horsetrading over portfolios, the responsibility for the conduct of CFSP was removed from Hans van den Broek and taken over by no less than the Commission President himself.

CFSP also has certain features which could take foreign policy cooperation far beyond what was possible in EPC, and which could have important effects upon multilateral management of defence-related trade within the EU. Comprehension of the scope of the CFSP provisions is often made difficult by the use of obscure and ambiguous language, but the TEU provides for three levels of intergovernmental cooperation in foreign policy and related fields, ranging from 'systematic cooperation' and 'common position' (both offered by TEU Art. J.2), to 'joint action' (offered by TEU Art. J.3). The first amounts to no more than agreement among the governments to 'inform and consult one another within the Council on any matter of foreign and security policy of general interest in order to ensure that their combined influence is exerted as effectively as possible by means of concerted and convergent action' (TEU Art. J.2.1).

In some circumstances, the Council of Ministers might move to the next level and agree unanimously upon a 'common position' to which national governments will be 'politically' (rather than legally) bound to conform (TEU Art. J.2.2). The third level, 'joint action', attempts to move beyond reactive declarations of opinion or preference. Joint action provides for a more integrated decision-making process, one which could enable the EU to behave more like a national government by projecting a coherent foreign policy, rather than merely responding to foreign developments. Thus, on the basis of 'general guidelines' agreed unanimously and issued by the European Council concerning the scope of CFSP, the Council of Ministers can decide (also unanimously) that certain matters should be subject to joint action and (again unanimously) that certain aspects of the joint action should be implemented by majority voting (TEU Art. J.3.1-2). The joint-action voting and implementation provisions have with some justification been described as a 'clumsy compromise'.[10]

In December 1992 at Edinburgh the European Council published its first set of guidelines. Under the sub-heading 'Economic Aspects of Security', certain arms export-related matters were listed as possible candidates for joint action: transparency in conventional arms transfers; the 'transparency in armaments' item on the agenda of the UN Conference on Disarmament; the follow-up to the UN Register of Conventional Arms; the adoption by the CSCE of common arms export criteria similar to the EPC criteria; and common licence revocation procedures and review of existing UN and European arms embargoes. What is most striking about the European Council document is its emphasis on transparency in arms exports (three out of the five items listed), an exercise which has so far proved to be low-cost and low-impact in political terms. The CSCE item resulted in the adoption in November 1993 by the Forum for Security Cooperation of a list of 'Principles and Guidelines' concerning conventional arms transfers; a document which has also so far defied gravity. The final item hardly represented a great advance; discussion of common licence-revocation procedures and embargoes was a familiar aspect of EPC. In late October 1993, days before the TEU entered into force, the first five joint actions were listed: the promotion of peace and security in Europe; the Middle East; former Yugoslavia; elections in Russia; and South Africa. Subsequent joint actions concerned the provision of humanitarian aid to Bosnia, the definition of an EU position at the Nuclear Non-Proliferation Treaty Review and Extension Conference in spring 1995, and a May 1995 moratorium on the export of anti-personnel land mines. The joint-action procedure was also used to draw up and publish the control lists relating to the EU dual-use regulation.

By introducing majority voting onto the hallowed ground of foreign policy, the joint-action process could be an important, and possibly far-reaching, innovation; 'perhaps the overriding success of the [TEU] that compensates for a whole range of more disappointing factors'.[11] But whatever its potential, for a number of reasons it is an innovation which is unlikely to have immediate effect. For as long as CFSP remains essentially an intergovernmental forum, it is doubtful that the tradition of unanimity, 'bred through decades of EPC',[12] will give way easily, and it will therefore obstruct majority voting. Often though, rather than push disagreement to the point at which the only recourse would be to block EPC decision-making by use of a national veto or, under CFSP, to persuade other member governments to resort to the heavy hand of majority voting, governments have instead accepted the mood of the apparent majority in order to ensure a 'unanimous' decision.[13] If, in spite of ostensible adherence to unanimity, intergovernmental working practice favours consensus over confrontation, then it is still more unlikely that majority voting will be much used. This could have one of two effects. Governments might be persuaded to seek common ground and 'build' consensus in difficult areas or, conversely, the outcome could be that those areas where confrontation is most likely would remain untried by the joint-action/majority-voting process. In the latter case, the outcome would be that majority agreements could be achieved only at the level of the lowest common denominator. Governments might find it useful to have agreement in certain peripheral policy areas, but the main incentive would be the symbolic value of agreements made relatively easily, with minimal political cost and disharmony; 'the maintenance of unity can take precedence over policy content resulting in a common position that lacks effective substance'.[14] Furthermore, since joint actions 'commit the Member States in the positions they adopt and in the conduct of their activity' (TEU Art. J.3.4), deviation from which could face legal challenge from other member states, in some areas some member governments might be reluctant to be pushed into a corner politically and legally, with the result that those policy areas would once again not be considered suitable for the joint-action process. Finally, with such a wide variety of subjects potentially suitable for joint action, in different categories of political importance, experience and difficulty, the joint action process cannot be uniform in implementation. Some joint actions will be easier to identify and implement than others. The South Africa joint action, for example, was built upon a high level of consensus in national policies towards South Africa and was thus relatively easy to agree.[15]

With the impending IGC in mind, governments began preparing position papers in early summer 1995. A 'reflection group' of national experts met in Messina, Italy in early June 1995 to begin drawing up an agenda for the IGC. The developing debate embraces several fundamental issues such as the rate at which the EU will take on new members from central and eastern Europe, the timetable for monetary union, and the degree to which the EU can function as an *à la carte* organization in which member states can determine their own terms of membership. Sharply differing national positions on these and other issues suggest that the debate will be vigorous, both before and during the IGC. Some governments take the view that the object of the 1996 IGC should be less a major redraft of the treaty than delicate 'fine-tuning' of the EU and its already ambitious agenda.[16] But the institutions of the EU have also provided position papers and a steady input to the debate, and tend to take a more far-reaching approach. In a Commission paper published in early May 1995, Santer caused concern in some national governments when he demanded more majority voting in CFSP. Santer's approach, and the Commission's generally unfavourable view of intergovernmentalism in foreign policy coordination, built upon an earlier report on CFSP commissioned by Hans van den Broek, the Commissioner for external political relations. The report condemned the 'inertia and impotence of the CFSP and WEU' as the 'inward and outward reflection of a lack of capacity or will to act, particularly as regards the threat and/or use of force by the Union'. The report went on to recommend a 'central capacity for analysis and planning' in all matters relating to CFSP and defence, and commented on the 'twin perils of blinkered concentration on hastily conceived "joint actions" on the one hand and sterile bureaucratisation on the other'.[17] The EP's position paper published in May 1995 also caused some controversy with its call to abolish the national veto in virtually all EU policy-making and legislation, including foreign, security and defence matters.

Prospects for cooperation in the management of defence-related trade will be determined by the fate of CFSP at the IGC. A number of outcomes are conceivable. First, the CFSP 'pillar', and with it the joint-action process, could collapse completely, with foreign, security and defence policy-making being completely 'renationalized'. This outcome would see the abandonment of any attempt at systematic cooperation in export controls. The most that could then be expected would be a return to *ad hoc*, reactive intergovernmental cooperation. While no doubt favoured by those 'Euro-sceptics' most anxious to limit supranationalism in the EU generally, this outcome is extremely unlikely. CFSP may have uncertain foundations, but it has become an established feature of the EU, largely because member governments have seen fit to cooperate, at different levels of sophistication, in a widening array of areas related to foreign and security policy. 'Spill-over' from cooperation in the CCP also makes it difficult to isolate 'high politics'; as Britain's foreign secretary remarked in October 1994, 'The question is not the need for cooperation but its *form*.'[18] This leaves at least the possibility of continuing with some form of cooperation in defence-trade matters. The second hypothesis lies at the opposite end of the spectrum and would see the merging of the EC and the two intergovernmental 'pillars'. In a fully integrated Union, the Commission would have, more than simply a voice, the exclusive right of initiative in foreign, security and defence matters. With the expansion of the EU to a membership of twenty or more states from western, central and eastern Europe, the integrationist school also argues for genuine majority voting in such matters. A fully integrated EU would mean supranational control of defence-related trade going far beyond anything yet achieved, or even attempted, in Europe and elsewhere. But given the high level of scepticism regarding the EU's performance and potential in these areas, scepticism which is unlikely to diminish by late 1996, this option too can be ruled unlikely.

A more probable fate for foreign policy cooperation within the EU is the continuation, possibly with some adjustments, of the existing CFSP system. CFSP currently offers a form of intergovernmental cooperation which is more systematic and formal than that which obtains in the judicial and home affairs 'pillar', but which falls short of the centralism and supranational authority of the EC. This median position, which could be described as 'enhanced intergovernmentalism', might see defence and security matters being detached from foreign policy cooperation and placed in a fourth, more clearly intergovernmental 'pillar'. But even if the basic structure of CFSP were to remain unchanged, there would still be potential for effective cooperation in defence-related trade. The full range of current CFSP cooperation would be available: information exchange, common position and joint action. By this latter view, rather than expect the character of CFSP, or the EU itself, to change so radically that a new, fully integrated approach to supply-side defence trade management could be possible, it is more prudent to ask where, in the spectrum offered by 'enhanced intergovernmentalism', defence trade management might find a home and whether it is reasonable to expect anything beyond peripheral, lowest-common-denominator agreements.

With CFSP and the joint-action process still in their infancy, it is too early to judge accurately where the political limits of export control cooperation in the EU might lie. The use of the joint-action process to clear the blockage over the dual-use regulation might in time prove to have been the first, cautious step towards closer integration. But for several reasons, more modest expectations are probably in order for the immediate future, with defence trade cooperation probably remaining at the less developed end of the range of CFSP options. It has already been shown that the agenda for joint action is very wide. The fact that joint actions have been possible in certain areas and functions does not indicate that the process will be applicable, to a uniform standard, across the whole agenda. Although there has clearly been a good deal of cooperation in matters associated with defence-related trade in the EU, the results of this cooperation have been limited and largely reactive. The ground may simply not be as fertile as that from which, for example, the South Africa joint action grew. To begin at a much lower level of cooperation, in an area of policy which has so far been fiercely guarded by governments, and to expect very much more than basic agreements, may therefore be too ambitious at present. In some respects, cooperation in defence-related trade has been so delicate and difficult that it was unwise to include it on the first joint-action agenda, giving credence to the claim discussed in Chapter 2 that the December 1992 Edinburgh European Council 'general guidelines' for joint actions only included arms export-related matters as a result of bureaucratic confusion over the 'Asolo List'.

That the joint-action process was never meant to be applied to defence-related matters, arguably including arms exports, is also suggested by Article J.4.3 of the TEU which states plainly that 'Issues having defence implications dealt with under this Article shall not be subject to the [joint-action] procedures set out in Article J.3.' Although the mandate for CFSP includes 'all questions related to the security of the Union, including the eventual framing of a common defence policy, which might in time lead to a common defence' (TEU Art. J.4.1), it would therefore appear that CFSP was not expected to be applied uniformly, in all relevant policy areas, from the outset. If defence industries could be described as vital strategic assets in terms of national defence and security, then it could be reasonable to extend the same logic to the arms exports which currently sustain those industries. This raises the intriguing possibility that the TEU contains within it something like an Article 223 limitation on the scope of CFSP, enabling member governments to cite 'defence implications' as a means to deflect the joint-action process away from defence-related areas. Article 223, it should be remembered, restricts EC involvement in 'the production of *or trade* in arms'. This apparent contradiction will be addressed at the 1996 IGC, until which point EU foreign ministers meeting in the the General Affairs Council have recommended that joint actions should not be 'explicitly' defence-related.

The broader question of the extension of EU cooperation into the fields of security and defence can never be far from the discussion of export control cooperation. Some of the long-standing prejudice against EU involvement in defence matters has given way recently. In the United States, the view that European defence cooperation could only under-mine NATO has softened, partly in the face of Congressional demands for Europe to shoulder more of the burden of its own defence and security affairs after the Cold War. A new mood is also indicated by France's gradual *rapprochement* with NATO's military structure since 1992,[19] and by Britain's 'change of tack' to support a 'European power bloc in Nato' in autumn 1994.[20] But whatever the possibilities for defence-related cooperation in the EU, several member governments are deter-mined that the process should remain unequivocally intergovernmental. During a speech in Brussels early in 1995, Britain's defence minister insisted that 'European defence and security should remain the preserve of EU governments alone – without any role for the Commission or the European Parliament.'[21] On a more emotional level, the possibility that armed forces might be asked to risk their lives for what might be described as a remote political process has also raised misgivings:

> More than any other policy field, security and defence strike at the heart of national sovereignty. For the foreseeable future none of the EC members can be expected to commit itself to majority decision-making or to accept the authority of a supranational body on questions of life and death.[22]

For as long as political, cultural and emotional considerations of this sort persist, 'enhanced intergovernmentalism' is the very most that might be expected, but even this may be too ambitious in certain policy areas. Ultimately, this inertia may only be overcome when member govern-ments decide that it is in their interests to do so. The history of the EU shows that governments have been willing to 'pool sovereignty' when analysis of the costs and benefits of cooperation point in that direction. But it is instructive to remember that at the beginning of EPC, the 'benefit' which governments sought was nothing more than 'a forum in which to exchange information and attempt to coordinate positions *without directly affecting their vested national interests*'.[23] Given the harshly competitive conditions of the international arms market and the lingering perception that defence manufacturing is above all a national asset which, for domestic political, industrial and strategic reasons, is best served by retaining a substantial degree of national control, it is not yet apparent that member governments will be willing to cooperate in defence-related trade in anything other than non-contentious and peripheral areas, and in a non-compulsory way. As Chapter 4 showed, although the 'national-champion' view of defence industry in Europe has many critics in government and industry, several key governments have yet to be convinced that the economic and industrial benefits of integrating arms exports and other defence industrial functions could offset the possible political costs of sharing political decision-making in these areas.

Chapter 6
Principles

Introduction

Previous chapters have shown that multilateral efforts to manage the international trade in conventional arms and technology have generally not been an unqualified success, particularly where west Europeans have been involved. It has proven difficult for arms supplier states to go much beyond relatively straightforward, reactive, punitive arms embargoes. Technological diffusion and the lack of cohesion among the suppliers help to explain this deficiency. But it is the possibility of a deeper, conceptual weakness in multilateral arms trade management which is the focus of this chapter. The first part of the chapter turns to fundamental questions; why should states in general wish to cooperate in the management of the arms market, and what types of cooperation are, or could be, available? The next step, in search of a central organizing principle, is to compare conventional arms export initiatives with more explicitly norm-driven WMD non-proliferation regimes. The third problem to address is whether conventional arms export policies can be directive and used as levers to modify the behaviour of clients, or indeed whether export decisions can be shaped at all by behavioural expectations assumed to be universally valid.

Cooperation in arms export controls: motives and means

To ask why states should wish to cooperate in regulating the arms trade begs a prior question; why is national regulation sought in the first place? Although it is true to say that many regulatory initiatives have been proposed on behalf of the international community, or humanity itself, it appears that a powerful sense of protecting or advancing national interest often lies at the heart of efforts to manage the arms trade multilaterally. National interest is an expression notoriously resistant to simple definition, but it is often in the name of this vague concept that governments cooperate and seek to achieve, or make more effective, their individual goals of management and supervision. These goals reflect various pragmatic, legal and ethical requirements and judgments.

The pragmatist might see that for as long as there has been a demand for weapons and military equipment there has also been interest in the conduct and consequences of any transactions, with regular intervention in the market place by those responsible for the production and supply of relevant goods and technology. Studies of the arms trade cite examples of intervention going as far back as the Middle Ages, with a brief phase of *laissez-faire* practice at the end of the nineteenth century seen as the exception to prove the general rule.[1] The essential quality of defence-related trade, which underpins most assessments of the economic, political, technological and strategic implications of a given transaction, and which drives governments to intervene, is that the trade involves the distribution of military power. By extension, the defence and even survival of governments, states and societies could be affected; 'trade in armaments ... [has] potential to affect a nation's security [assuring] its treatment as a phenomenon uniquely relevant to world politics'.[2] The pragmatist's perspective, therefore, amounts to the claim that it must be in the interest of governments to avoid possible adverse consequences of defence-related trade by controlling the trade and the market place.

As far as proliferation and arms exports are concerned, national governments are both the primary source and the agent of international law, and are required by that law to have the means to supervise and regulate the arms trade. In some circumstances, unregulated arms sales and transfers could amount to illegal intervention or even outright aggression. The international community of states having agreed, in the UN Charter and various Security Council and General Assembly resolutions, to join in preventing such transgressions, it follows that states have an obligation to cooperate in arms trade regulation.[3] Having agreed in Article 2.5 of the Charter to 'give the [UN] every assistance in any action it takes', all UN member states are committed to 'refrain from giving assistance to any state against which the [UN] is taking preventive or enforcement action' and to 'establish standing mechanisms for the national regulation of their arms exports in order to be in a position to enforce mandatory arms embargoes'.[4] Embargoes are not the only issue, however. States must meet a variety of obligations in international law, such as not supporting terrorist groups, and this requires all states to have the means to supervise and control any transfer of arms, ammunition and military equipment, whatever the circumstances of the transaction.[5] Some arms control and disarmament treaties have required states to manage the redistribution of military equipment. The 1990 Conventional Armed Forces in Europe Treaty (CFE), for example, was an elaborate agreement to reduce the numbers of conventional forces deployed in Europe by NATO and the Warsaw Pact.[6] With large amounts of high-quality military equipment about to be dismantled or destroyed, NATO's response was to implement an 'Equipment Transfer and Rationalization Programme'. The programme, also known as 'cascade', was designed to ensure that NATO allies could upgrade their arsenals with advanced, surplus stock while at the same meeting the overall reduction commitments made in the CFE treaty.[7] International humanitarian law, or the laws of war, can also require governments to cooperate in restricting the supply of certain weapons.

Mention of the laws of war introduces the moral dimension to the discussion. Humanitarian law stigmatizes certain military practices and weapons as inhumane, indiscriminate or disproportionate. As the recent campaign against anti-personnel landmines illustrates, arguments from this perspective can have a powerful influence on defence-related trade.[8] It is, of course, not just the conduct of war which raises ethical objections and questions: 'For the Christian non-pacifist, as for the pacifist, this is not an industry like any other. Selling weapons is not exclusively an economic issue.'[9] Discussion of the ethics of defence-related trade is often rather entrenched. At one extreme lies the argument that weapons are morally neutral, that 'weapons do not make war, people do'. The bitter conflict over the separation of India and Pakistan in 1947 is often cited as evidence of destruction, killing and cruelty on a vast scale achieved without the benefit of modern weaponry. Events in Rwanda in 1994 provide a more recent illustration of the same argument. By this argument, moral concern about the transfer or possession of certain types of weapons is a misplaced and self-indulgent obsession with technology; the only proper subject for moral examination is the intention of the maker, owner or buyer of the weapon. In any case, the argument might continue, it is difficult to define and sustain objective moral criteria. Important general principles, such as the need to enable states to defend against aggression, or even the need to deny arms to oppressive regimes, may prove to be less than universally and eternally valid and beg many secondary questions which can only be answered in context. There is, for example, no universal agreement on what makes an appropriate or 'legitimate' level of self-defence, and a convincing definition of 'aggression' has so far eluded the UN. Defence-related trade, the argument might conclude, therefore takes place in a moral vacuum; there may be reasons why governments should intervene in the arms trade, but morality is not one of them.

At the other extreme lies the proposition that defence-related trade is more causative than symptomatic of conflict and is therefore an ethical issue in its own right. Interwar reaction against the 'merchants of death' who, allegedly, fuelled the 1914–18 war, illustrates this thinking, as does the currently popular analogy between defence-related trade and the illegal trade in narcotics, with talk of tackling the 'arms pushers' who corrupt and manipulate their 'victims'.[10] The proposition extends into the notion that certain machines and technologies, far from being morally 'neutral', can be described as 'offensive' or 'destabilizing' and should therefore be banned or subject to special controls. As the basis for informed, balanced decisions on defence-related trade, each of these alternatives is as 'simplistic and inadequate' as the other.[11] The first approach suggests either that the international system is reducible to a Darwinian free-for-all, or that officials and policy-makers are just impotent ciphers, trapped in a 'Greek tragedy, the tragedy of necessity, where the feeling aroused in the spectator is "What a pity it had to be this way"'.[12] However, even the most convinced adherent of *Realpolitik* will at some point be drawn into making ethical judgments: 'The notion of "national interest" is based upon the values of the national community, values which can be regarded as the product of its culture and as the expression of its sense of cohesion, values which define for men what they believe to be right or just.'[13] Yet the alternative suggestion that mankind is being obstructed, by arms traders and even some machines, from achieving a natural state of global harmony seems to go too far at a time when aggressors, dictators and other unsavoury characters plainly exist. The ethical debate on defence-related trade may be doomed to vacillate fruitlessly between these irreconcilable positions, and may as a result offer little in terms of policy advice. What is certain, however, is that much of the pressure exerted on Western governments by their electorates will stem from general, ethically motivated disquiet about the conduct and consequences of defence-related trade.

For a variety of pragmatic, legal and moral reasons, therefore, governments on the supply side of defence-related trade are motivated or pressurized to manage their involvement in the market. All states involved in the trade have developed some sort of management system, and it is at this unilateral level that most management of defence-related trade has taken place.[14] Some analysts argue that the trend towards multi-lateralism is misplaced, and that efforts at the unilateral level offer the only real possibility of control.[15] But governments, aware of the diversity of the global market and of the spread of manufacturing capability, and conscious that the internationalization of defence industry, notably in western Europe, implies the need for some form of multilateral management, are nevertheless drawn to multilateral cooperation in managing defence-related trade. Yet as the number of manufacturers, suppliers and purchasers increases, so it becomes necessary to involve more and more governments in any regulatory initiative if success is to be achieved, and the practical and political obstacles to effective cooperation accordingly become higher. Particularly when certain of the vigorous new arms exporters have acquired their capability in spite of the best efforts of the original suppliers, then, for as long as they retain their 'pariah' status, it is unlikely that they would be willing to cooperate in regulating the arms trade. In other words, as the need to cooperate becomes more pronounced, so the scope for effective cooperation can diminish.

When governments decide, for whatever reason, that the management of defence-related trade could best be achieved in concert, a number of options present themselves. The simplest conceivable form of export control cooperation would be that which takes place on an *ad hoc* basis, as circumstances required, and which results in jointly implemented arms or technology embargoes. With no attempt to organize the cooperation in any formal or institutional way, and no attempt to justify the cooperation through an appeal to a higher political or moral authority, initiatives of this sort might best be described as reactive, concerted, militant diplomacy. Such agreements, made at short notice and for a short period, might be relatively easy to make and could have a rapid effect, both on domestic public opinion and on the 'target' state. But *ad hoc* initiatives involving just a few like-minded states might also prove easy for the participants to leave, and equally easy for the targets to evade. Governments are accordingly persuaded both that cooperation should have some form of organization, and that the initiative should include as many of the relevant suppliers and recipients as possible or appropriate. Another consideration might be that governments which appeared too willing to implement unilateral, *ad hoc* embargoes might become known to the demand side as politically and commercially unreliable. The relationship between supply and demand can never be guaranteed. This applies in all areas of industry and commerce, including the trade in arms and technology, particularly when 'buyer's market' conditions prevail. In these circumstances, governments might wish to legitimize their action by, say, a UN Security Council Resolution or by appealing to universalist ideals such as the advancement of human rights. What is more, with research, development and training times often lasting well over a decade, it is generally thought necessary to take a long view when considering how, and for how long, to restrict the arms and technology trade. Cooperation in the management of defence-related trade therefore suggests three desiderata. First, the initiative will seek to be organized and institutionalized, rather than appear merely a casual arrangement between governments. Second, the participants will draw upon a higher authority rather than appear to be driven by mere *Realpolitik* and national interest. Legal and political authority might come from the UN, while moral authority might come from religious conviction or from adherence to other universalist ideals. Finally, the initiative is likely to take place over time rather than appear spontaneous and short-lived.

When cooperation between states becomes deliberate and prescriptive, and where a formal or semi-formal organization is sought, so it becomes appropriate to think in terms of 'regimes'. The creation, maintenance and consequences of regimes have received a great deal of attention in academic writing on international relations. By one popular definition, international regimes amount to 'principles, norms, rules and decision-making procedures around which actor expectations converge in a given issue-area'.[16] Casual, *ad hoc* cooperation in the management of defence-related trade, of the sort referred to earlier, would be described as 'short-term calculations of interest', and would therefore not qualify as regimes. Instead, regimes involve 'some sense of general obligation',[17] and this must be manifested over time. Where the object of the regime is to manage defence-related trade, the 'sense of general obligation' could, but need not necessarily, exclude the state or states which are or which become the target of the regime. By one account, regimes are quintessentially 'hegemonic structures ... in which the rules are clear and obeyed' and are therefore best seen as a legacy of the Cold War.[18] Although too much can be expected from elegant theorizing, regime theory does nevertheless help to explain the modes of formal cooperation open to governments.

Cooperation in the control of defence-related trade might be achieved in one of two ways. The key to the first, the enforced or hegemonic trade-management regime, is that the norm or 'sense of general obligation' is agreed by the suppliers but not accepted by the recipients or targets. There are two variants of this type of initiative. The first variant is a relatively straightforward matter of denial and domination, the best example of which would be the conditions imposed on a defeated state. Rather more subtle, and much more complex, enforcement can also be a matter of drawn-out, systematic trade restrictions such as the CoCom initiative of 1949–94 and, more recently, the various WMD technology-transfer control regimes such as the NSG and the MTCR. The second variant could be described as 'hegemony by stealth', where access to arms or technology becomes, more than a matter of foreign policy or commerce, a process of *de facto* hegemony through 'leadership and the manipulation of incentives'.[19] Clients might be required to accept certain conditions regarding their overall military expenditure, their relations with neighbouring states, their support for arms control initiatives and even the character of their society and government in exchange for access to the market. Generally, aid conditionality is not a novel concept and features regularly in current debates on foreign aid and demilitariza-tion. In their July 1991 'Declaration on Conventional Arms Transfers and NBC Non-Proliferation', the Group of Seven industrialized demo-cracies agreed that donor countries should 'take account of military expenditure where it is disproportionate when setting up aid pro-grammes'.[20] Making foreign aid and investment conditional on the be-haviour of the recipients is a controversial subject. Yet when conditionality tactics are employed in the arms and sensitive-technology trade, not only does the familiar contradiction emerge between market opportunism and market regulation, but the idea also appears to assume a degree of consensus, both among suppliers and between suppliers and recipients, which is unlikely given post-Cold War market conditions.[21]

The second broad approach is to seek the 'consensual regime', one which is genuinely multilateral, involving suppliers as well as recipients, and which is based upon a universal or at least widely held set of norms and values. The various initiatives to prevent the proliferation of nuclear, biological and chemical weapons would fall into this category although, as suggested earlier, some features of these regimes (such as the export control arrangements) appear to have more in common with supply-side exclusivity. The presumption against horizontal proliferation of WMD transcended the Cold War confrontation and still has a considerable international constituency. Complacency in this regard may, however, be increasingly misplaced. Since the end of the Cold War there have been several instances of acquisition and even use of WMD in obvious contravention of the various regimes. But maverick WMD research and development programmes are hardly a new phenomenon and to some extent serve to emphasize the general non-proliferation norm. What may prove far more hazardous is the possible erosion of this general norm among more responsible states and governments. The difficulties in negotiating the review and extension of the Nuclear Non-Proliferation Treaty and the unhurried ratification of the Chemical Weapons Convention may indicate a loss of faith in the blanket presumption against WMD proliferation.

However vulnerable the WMD non-proliferation regimes are becoming, they are still considerably more solid and durable than anything which might be called a norm against conventional proliferation. It is not easy to transfer WMD non-proliferation ideas and practices to the conventional area; while there are 'unambiguous ethical, pragmatic and power-political' reasons to prevent nuclear proliferation, and 'considerable international acceptance' of those reasons, 'in the area of conventional arms there are no such unambiguous answers.'[22] By this view, the best that might be hoped for is a global regime to ban the production and trade in particularly inhumane or brutal weapons. To the extent that the law of war, and even international law in general, is but the sum of the will of the international community of states, then humanitarian and legal restraints upon the international arms trade could themselves be described as a 'consensual regime'.

In pursuit of an international conventional arms trade norm

There is wide agreement in the literature as to the difficulty of establishing and maintaining a set of general norms or values which might govern the transfer of conventional weapons and related technology. Some hope has been expressed that the December 1991 UN Register of Conventional Arms might be the first step towards the creation of a globally respected body of values,[23] but international support for the Register has been slow to develop. Governments are pushed, for a variety of reasons, towards some form of multilateral regulation of the arms trade. Yet this impulse has so far had limited effect. The complex task of balancing commercial, political and moral considerations would doubtless be facilitated by the identification of a principle or code by which to shape difficult decisions nationally and multilaterally. It may equally be that no such value exists or could ever be identified, or that the norm being sought is no less than one which could deal with aggression, conflict and war itself. In any case, the search for such a code has so far been of more interest to analysts of the international arms trade than to participants in it. This is in part attributable to the character of the post-Cold War arms market, which emphasizes a competitive, non-cooperative commercial logic and which makes it difficult even for like-minded suppliers to define common goals and rules by which to regulate their participation in the arms trade.

Beyond commercial considerations, other explanations might be offered for this dilemma. The end of the Cold War adversarial relationship has removed one important source of structure and control. The hegemonic, or 'spheres of influence', character of Cold War arms trading has been replaced by what might be termed the 'Article 51 argument', one which seems singularly unlikely to produce the elusive norm. Article 51 of the UN Charter guarantees each state's 'inherent right of individual or collective self-defence'. As the British government and others have argued, Article 51 implies that states have 'the right to acquire the means with which to defend themselves.'[24] Comments to this effect were included in several of the post-Cold War regulatory initiatives launched in 1991. If self-defence is a key attribute of sovereignty, the argument might continue, then any interference in the right to self-defence, for example by instituting an arms embargo, undermines the notion of national sovereignty, one of the key features of the international system. Since national sovereignty is an attribute which the 'interferers' also enjoy and would be unwilling to surrender, and since their 'interfering' is usually done in the name of an international system built upon the concept of national sovereignty, it can be seen that the 'Article 51 argument' does some damage to the search for a central organizing value. It is also possible that governments have become conditioned to see conventional arms transfers as a peripheral issue, if not normal or even preferred practice. This conditioning could be seen as a legacy of the Cold War, when WMD arms control and non-proliferation tended to capture the greater part of government and public imagination. Given East-West tension, this bias was reasonable but it had the effect of relegating conventional arms transfer controls to the second order and even meant that conventional arms transfers became a 'release valve', or a means to continue the Cold War struggle by other, non-WMD means. The WMD/conventional substitution issue remains relevant today, in that an over-restrictive arms trade regime which had the effect of pushing the 'target' state down the path of WMD acquisition would probably be seen as counterproductive.

The diffuse post-Cold War international order, combined with a legacy of relative indifference to the spread of conventional weapons, seems to offer three choices, none of them especially convincing as a guiding principle. First, the 'Article 51 argument' could be taken to mean that the international arms trade can only be judged in relative or regional terms; an overarching or absolute set of values is logically, politically and morally unattainable. A second choice could be to apply the Cold War 'release valve' idea and argue that the international arms trade ought still, in certain circumstances, to be encouraged. The priority would be to ensure that states are not persuaded that their goals could be realized through the acquisition of WMD. This argument could also extend into the idea that states have a moral obligation to sell arms to those engaged in self-defence against an aggressor. There is a compelling simplicity to both the 'Article 51' and the 'release valve' arguments, but since both entail a presumption of access to the arms market rather than restraint of it, it appears that the pragmatic, legal and moral considerations which prompt states to wish to control the market would have to be compromised in some way. A third option could be to argue that while self-defence is indeed a right of states, it is a right which must be enjoyed within the rule-based international legal and political system. More importantly, one state's right to self-defence should not entail an unqualified moral and legal obligation on other states to export weapons, except where there is a treaty requirement to assist or defend allies.[25] But if the best that can be said is that 'decisions must be made', then the third option is hardly more than a restatement of the problem, rather than a solution to it.

Trade in conventional arms and technology differs from WMD proliferation in three other respects. First, although the risks which may accompany the acquisition of a large conventional arsenal ought not to be underestimated, these risks are best understood in local or at most regional terms. This same complacency could, however, prove to be wholly misplaced with regard to the acquisition by some states of WMD. Nuclear, biological and chemical weaponry, and ballistic missiles, have been described as 'catastrophic weaponry', weapons which would, if used, 'necessarily devastate civilian populations with catastrophic consequences'.[26] Simply put: 'the global threat from states acquiring more conventional arms is qualitatively different from that of the same states acquiring nuclear armaments'.[27]

The second distinction lies in the character of the weapons. WMD are often perceived and described in absolute terms, strategically, politically, legally and morally. These perceptions have so far exerted a powerful influence upon decisions regarding the development, possession and possible use of WMD. But the same might not be said of conventional weapons. The manufacture, ownership and deployment of conventional weapons are more readily understood to be a function of a given political and military context, rather than directive of it.[28] Although it must be correct to say that in some circumstances, certain weapons can be 'destabilizing' or offer an 'offensive' capability, it is particularly difficult to apply such judgments in a categorical way where conventional weapons are concerned. The technical capabilities of a given conventional weapon system are available to the possessor to exploit, in aggression as in defence; 'destabilizing' and 'offensive' are therefore judgments which can only be made in context. For a military commander in a defensive position, the vital task is to steal the initiative from the aggressor, and 'offensive' weapons such as tanks could be used legitimately for this purpose. A conventional confrontation is often as much about the initiative and ability of the military commander as it is about the quantity and quality of the weapons being deployed. On many occasions, being on equal terms in armaments, or even being the underdog, has had little bearing on military decisions. Indeed, some military commanders appear to view qualitative and quantitative disadvantage as a challenge to be met, and rather relish acting the role of David outsmarting Goliath. The performance of the Israeli armed forces on the Golan Heights in 1973 is often cited in this respect, but a more recent example of the triumph of self-confidence over military capability might be the Chechen rebels' struggle against Russian armour and air power in late 1994 and 1995. It is also relevant to note that US and NATO military doctrine underwent a 'revolution' in the 1980s and early 1990s, the result of which is a deliberate blurring of offensive and defensive in military planning and operations.[29]

The final distinction between the conventional arms trade and WMD proliferation is one which recalls the precepts of academic international regime theory on the one hand, and the facts of a diffuse and possibly uncontrollable worldwide conventional arms and technology production base on the other. As the production base broadens so it must become more difficult to control: 'multilateral efforts at controls can be effective only when the objects of controls are wholly within the influence orbit of those seeking to implement them'.[30] On a more theoretical level, diffusion also undermines one of the principles of effective non-proliferation; that 'deviants' should be kept 'small in number, isolated, and manageable'.[31]

These practical and theoretical stipulations might be relevant in the field of WMD proliferation, but they are largely inappropriate for the post-Cold War conventional arms market.

Cultural relativism

If there are practical and logical difficulties in establishing regimes by which the conventional arms and technology trade might be controlled, and if the norms and values upon which such regimes might be based appear particularly hard to identify, a related problem lies in the way such attempts at regime-building are viewed by both non-participants in, and targets of, the regime. The problem becomes most pronounced when the arms and technology recipients with the most awkward questions are at the same time enjoying the benefits of a buyer's market.

It has been suggested earlier in this chapter that a basic tension exists between the goal of arms trade regulation on one hand, and the principles of state sovereignty and non-intervention on the other. This tension might be caricatured in the following way. If self-defence and, by extension, the arms trade are attributes of sovereignty then a state should expect to be treated by its peers as 'innocent until proven guilty'; that is, to be allowed to exercise its self-defence and arms purchasing rights until good reason emerges why it should not. The tension mounts when the machinery of regulation is linked in some way to what is perceived to be the furtherance of the regulators' interests and values, which may be described by the regulators as universal values, but not accepted as such by the recipients or by other supplier governments. The tension is greatest when the linkage becomes prescriptive, and the regulators' values are presented as norms and standards to which all states should aspire. Of the various post-Cold War attempts to supervise or control the conventional arms trade, the UN Register of Conventional Arms emerges as the most neutral and even-handed, and the least judgmental. But the UN Register is more a supervisory than a regulatory initiative and has not yet, in any case, achieved general international support. The 'Permanent Five' and Group of Seven initiatives of 1991, however, went beyond the goal of restricting aggression and breaches of international peace and security to use such expressions as 'legitimate self-defence' when referring to potential recipients. From the recipient's point of view, expressions of this nature could imply that the right of self-defence has become less an attribute of state sovereignty, one which could be described as absolute and inalienable within the parameters of international law, than a quality which can be defined, awarded or denied by a group of states in the international system. The CSCE's November 1993 'Principles Governing Conventional Arms Transfers' went one step further and mentioned 'the respect for human rights and fundamental freedoms in the recipient country', as well as 'legitimate security and defence needs', as criteria against which potential conventional arms purchasers should be judged. The European Union's eight 'criteria', listed in the Appendix, present some of the same thinking. And in 1995, in a similar vein, the International Committee of the Red Cross began to investigate the possibility of linking arms transfer decisions to a potential recipient's compliance with the international humanitarian law of armed conflict.

With relatively clear and convincing sets of norms having been developed to accompany the various WMD non-proliferation initiatives, there is a strong temptation to assume that something similar ought to be available in the sphere of conventional arms and technology transfers. Yet the search for such a code is invariably contentious, and begs fundamental questions. Which is the main, organizing principle in the international system – the supposed universality of interests and values perceived by many to be characteristically Western, or the sovereign authority of individual states? Are ideas such as human rights and democracy universal, and universally applicable, values? The facts of the buyer's market, and the logic of the 'Article 51 argument', make it possible for recipient states to challenge the practice of 'hegemony by stealth', as they might perceive it. But there is a growing school of thought which argues that the imposition of conditions regarding human rights, democracy, and so forth are unacceptable because these are essentially Western, Judaeo-Christian values and concerns, rather than any universal standard. Even if they were acceptable as universal values, some would argue that they are ideals rather than policy prescriptions and that some states will require much more time to work towards these ideals while remaining stable and secure. In early 1995 a US Institute for National Security Studies report noted that while 'the global advancement of democracy and respect for human rights' had made 'notable strides' in the 1980s, the experience of the 1990s and the immediate prospects were less encouraging.[32] Although conditions were generally improving around the world, the report noted that 'democratic ideals' were in some cases being observed only perfunctorily. Since the end of the Cold War, these ideals had come under 'severe pressure' in many of the 'new democracies'. In some cases, the explanation was to be found in a clash of priorities:

Many new democracies have discovered problems in reconciling group rights and individual freedom with political stability. Severe contractions of national economies have frequently turned public opinion against democratic reformers who were raised to leadership in the wake of the Soviet Union's disintegration, most notably in Russia itself.

Other explanations offered in the report for the uneven application of democratic principles include the surge in nationalist feeling, awakened by improvements in communications and education, the close connection in some areas between political and religious movements, and the belief that religion, ethnicity and 'group consensus' are values which matter more than democratic ambitions. But the report also argued that the spread of democracy had in some senses been too successful, that democratic values had been spread too thin, and that 'with the global diffusion of democracy, it has become clear that what is meant by "democracy" varies from state to state as a result of differing cultural influences.'

The authors of the *Strategic Assessment* may have been influenced by two publications which appeared in 1993 and which received a great deal of attention thereafter. In the first, an article by Samuel Huntington, broadly similar assumptions of cultural relativism were explored, but on a global scale.[33] Huntington argued that the bases of future conflict would be primarily cultural, rather than ideological. He presented an image of a non-Western world whose peoples and governments were no longer willing to be 'the objects of history as the targets of Western colonialism' but would join the West as 'movers and shapers of history'.[34] Huntington found that the West had made use of ill-defined notions such as 'world community' and 'universal civilization' to legitimize the spread of Western values and preferences, political, economic and moral. Not only was the idea of a universal civilization at odds with 'the particularism of most Asian societies', but the values being presented also differed 'fundamentally' from those found in other civilizations: 'Western ideas of individualism, liberalism, constitutionalism, human rights, equality, liberty, the rule of law, democracy, free markets, the separation of church and state, often have little resonance in Islamic, Confucian, Japanese, Hindu, Buddhist or Orthodox cultures'.[35] Huntington also applied his 'clashing civilizations' thesis to the spread of conventional arms and technology. While most Western countries were reducing military spending and military power, many in the Middle East and Asia-Pacific regions were increasing theirs and asserting their 'right to acquire and to deploy whatever weapons they think necessary for their security'. In response to this loss of control, Huntington saw the West attempting to use arms control – 'a Western concept and a Western goal' – along with political and economic pressure to prevent the development of 'military capabilities that could threaten Western interests'. For their part, the states of the Middle East and the Asia-Pacific rim were developing a 'Confucian-Islamic military connection ... designed to promote acquisition by its members of the weapons and weapons technologies needed to counter the military power of the West.'[36]

If, in Huntington's view, cultural differences are the new determinants of international politics and an important explanation of the character of the post-Cold War arms trade, broadly similar things might be said of warfare itself, as in John Keegan's *A History of Warfare*, also published in 1993. Keegan found that warfare could only be understood in relative terms, as an expression of cultural structures and preferences. He found the resort to war, and conduct in war, to be a subject rather more complex and diffuse than the Clausewitzian model so popular in the West:

> Culture is ... a prime determinant of the nature of warfare, as the history of its development in Asia clearly demonstrates. Oriental warmaking, if we may so identify and denominate it as something different and apart from European warfare, is characterised by traits peculiar to itself ... Future peacekeepers and peacemakers have much to learn from alternative military cultures, not only that of the Orient, but of the primitive world also.[37]

A sense of cultural relativism might therefore be useful for those seeking to describe and understand the modern, post-Cold War world, and might help to explain some of the shortfalls noted in the *Strategic Assessment* report. At the simplest level, cultural relativism suggests that Western values and practices cannot after all be considered universal, but have to be placed alongside other, equally respectable and valid systems. Cultural relativism also, self-evidently, undermines the very notion of universalism itself. The tensions and contradictions which follow from this observation can be seen in the realm of international law. To the extent that the primary element of the international political system is the sovereign state, admitting of no superior secular authority or 'world government', then the system could be described as anarchic. But, in the sense conveyed by the expression 'anarchical society', the relations between the primary elements of the system conform to predictable patterns and are governed by rules.[38] Some international lawyers see themselves, therefore, not as practitioners of a supervening rule of law in the domestic sense, but as advocates of a cooperative, contractual law between states. In this sense, international law has been defined as 'the record of restrictions on sovereignty accepted by states', with its 'principle function' being to 'overcome the initial presumption of sovereignty and nonintervention'.[39]

But the fact that states are willing to enter into contractual relationships with each other – a minimalist definition of international law – should not be taken as evidence that all international or universal concepts will be treated with the same respect or in the same way. Nowhere is this more apparent than when concepts such as human rights, individual freedoms and democracy come into discussion. It might be thought that the Western origins of these ideas would wholly prejudice their wider acceptance, but the reality is more complex. Although human rights is by definition a universalist idea, and might therefore be rejected from the outset in some quarters, most states have accepted international definitions of the term, and have even agreed to be bound in international treaty law. This suggests that in certain cases universalism is not necessarily unacceptable. The distinction to be drawn is that whereas international law is to a large extent an expression of state sovereignty, concepts such as human rights and democracy are more clearly perceived to cut across and intrude upon that sovereignty because they are perceived to be more normative. The untidy outcome is that although states may have agreed upon definitions of human rights, some reserve the right, as sovereign members of the international community, to decide where, when and by whom these political goals should be realized. Unlike international law which is, in some respects, the servant of sovereignty, 'The universality of human rights fits uncomfortably in a political order structured around sovereign states.'[40]

In response to this dilemma, it may be necessary to adopt a compromise offered by such expressions as 'weak cultural relativism' and 'relative universality'.[41] It may also prove necessary to embark upon the abstract exercise of distinguishing between *absolute* and *universal*:

> we must reject the absurd test the Enlightenment imposed on religious and moral beliefs, namely that only if they were *universal* could they be *true*. As anthropologists began to uncover the full diversity of human behaviour, philosophers drew the conclusion that since

many of our deepest convictions about humanity were not universal,
they must be false. This is a fallacy and deserves to be challenged.[42]

But as far as the international market for arms and related technology is
concerned, the awkward reality which cannot be avoided is that many
non-Western countries now feel themselves in a position to decide, on
their own terms and for their own applications, what is meant by human
rights, freedom and good government. Thus, in May 1993, at about the
time Huntington's article appeared, Asian nations assembled in Bangkok
to issue a new definition of human rights, one which stressed social
stability and economic development over individual freedoms. Ideas of
this sort continue to be heard, particularly in the Asia-Pacific region and
in Southeast Asia. Malaysia's prime minister, Mahathir Mohamad, has
become an especially outspoken critic of Western attempts to proselytize:

> No one, no country, no people and no civilisation has a right to claim
> it has a monopoly of wisdom as to what constitute human rights ...
> [Western liberals] have no right at all to talk of human rights, much
> less judge others on this issue ... The record of the democratic
> governments of the West is not very inspiring. Unless their own
> interests are at stake, as in Kuwait, they would not risk anything in
> the cause of democracy. Is it any wonder that many countries are
> leery of the liberal system propounded by the Western democrats?[43]

Mahathir earlier gained notoriety for his angry response to British media
accusations regarding the Pergau Dam 'trade and aid' scandal. In a letter
to the *Financial Times*, Mahathir declared that 'Malaysians are not
concerned about British scruples over selling arms ... If you have scruples,
don't sell arms at all.'[44] In July 1995 Malaysia was one of the leading
Organization of Islamic Conference states to declare the UN arms embargo
on Bosnia invalid, and to offer military supplies to aid the Bosnian
Muslims.[45] Malaysia's close neighbour Singapore, also with close ties
with the West, has been similarly critical. Outcry following the legal case
in which the *International Herald Tribune* was found guilty of contempt
of court prompted Singapore's High Commissioner in London to publish
his view that 'democracy is a long process and, in the short term, it is
better perhaps to have more prosperity than democracy', and to note that
'Dogmatic assertions that Western democracy will inevitably triumph
over Asian values only reminds Asians of the fervour with which Com-
munists once proclaimed the inevitable triumph of Communism.'[46] And

following the collapse of a British merchant bank in March 1995, the same High Commissioner chastised *The Economist* for assuming that 'London bankers are the only people who have the integrity and ability to regulate and operate foreign exchanges. When a vulnerable British bank collapses it is not wise to blame it on regulatory failure on the part of your former colonial subjects – and their institutions – without checking the facts. Hubris indeed.'[47] The PRC has long argued along these lines. For the PRC, sovereignty and non-intervention have always been declared to be the basis of relations between states. Thus, in January 1995, following a US report on human rights abuses in the PRC, the Chinese response was to argue that 'The human rights issue is within the scope of the sovereignty of a country. Every country has the right to protect and promote human rights in accordance with its own situation.'[48] By one account, even the PRC's radical intellectuals had come to accept that the military crackdown in June 1989 was necessary and were supportive of Deng Xiaoping's view that the Soviet Union's attempt to achieve economic liberalization and political liberalism simultaneously was not an example which the PRC should attempt to follow.[49]

If, as is apparent from arguments of the sort advanced by Malaysia, Singapore and the PRC, the universal and unconditional acceptance of predominantly Western standards cannot be assumed, then it follows that political arrangements which draw upon – or merely make reference to – these standards could also be open to challenge. In these circumstances, discussion of the universality of human rights and democratic values could become an abstract and possibly counterproductive preoccupation. If the arrangement is one which simply and explicitly requires states to meet Western preferred standards of behaviour before, for example, commercial relationships can develop, then it is open for non-Western states to choose whether to comply with or reject that requirement, just as it is open for Western states to make such stipulations in the first instance. But these same standards assume a more rigid, prescriptive and controversial air when they are presented as universal values. At best, the outcome might be reduced scope for successful commercial relationships between states with different cultural systems. At worst, the outcome could be a perception of Western proselytizing and 'hegemony by stealth'; a tacit attempt to undermine national sovereign authority.

The West/North still has some means to compel Third World and developing countries to behave in certain ways, usually by attaching conditions to aid and investment provisions. And for the most egregious offences against Western opinion and standards of behaviour there are various types of embargo and economic sanction, and even military action. But arms transfer controls have not been a great success as a tool of coercive diplomacy,[50] and coercion hardly seems the stuff of which a global arms trade ethic and code of conduct could be made. Furthermore, as the Asia-Pacific region and Southeast Asia become ever more technologically and commercially dynamic and wealthy, and therefore attractive to Western investors, so it seems increasingly unwise for the West to insist upon the transcendence of values and standards which its potential commercial partners evidently do not share. Western self-confidence is least appropriate in the case of conventional-arms and technology transfers. Networks of arms sales and weapons development projects already stretch from the Middle East to the Asia-Pacific rim. With the inauguration in January 1995 of the Malaysia-Singapore Defence Forum, one object of which will be to enhance defence industrial collaboration between the two countries, and with Singapore also apparently offering defence industrial management expertise to the PRC,[51] it would appear that something similar to Huntington's 'Islamic-Confucian' connection could indeed be developing. In these circumstances, attempts by the West, or by the so-called 'supply side', to make conventional arms and technology transfers conditional could be viewed as culturally and morally arrogant and could prove to be commercially counterproductive. The eight EU arms export criteria appear to run precisely this risk. Adopting a wilfully contrary position, it could be argued that all but one of the criteria either assume the universality of standards and practices which may simply not be accepted, or assume for the EU the right to make judgments on the behaviour and concerns of other states. Only the fifth criterion, which refers to the national security demands of EU member states, could be said to make neither implicit nor explicit demands on the behaviour of the EU's conventional arms and technology clients.

Chapter 7

Conclusion

This study has focused on attempts by a group of arms- and technology-exporting states to cooperate in regulating their international trading activities. Historically, international efforts to reduce – or merely manage – the global trade in conventional weapons, equipment and related technology have had a patchy record and have proved difficult to sustain. Multilateral arms and technology embargoes, or restricted access regimes, have been used frequently, sometimes to great effect. But conventional arms embargoes and the like have been seen to be contingent phenomena, shaped more by changing political and strategic circumstances than by the possibly more durable, but rather less tangible, notion of the disinterested will of the 'international community'. For 45 years after the end of the Second World War, the international arms trade was dominated by the East-West confrontation, and the trade expanded dramatically during these years. As far as regulation is concerned, the best that might be said of the Cold War is that it imposed some sense of order on the international arms market. The 1990s have seen rapid contraction in the global market from the postwar peak in the late 1980s. But in the absence even of the rudimentary discipline of the Cold War, with the spread of arms manufacturing and technological capability, and with the arrival of a buyer's market for conventional military equipment and related technology, the shrinking market of the 1990s has become less ordered and predictable. Accordingly, recent initiatives to bring the arms trade under some form of international control look set to share the fate of similar attempts made earlier this century. Against this unpromising backgound, this study assesses the potential of the members and institutions of the European Union as managers of a sizeable share of the international arms trade, and asks whether the patchy record of multilateral regulation might now be improved.

The unique political and legal structure of the EU requires different approaches to be taken to controlling the export of conventional weapons on the one hand, and related technology on the other. Chapters 2 and 3 show how these different problems have been addressed since 1945. In both cases the key to effective multilateral cooperation has been the existence of functioning national export control systems. All current members of the EU have developed complex national arrangements in recent years, although standards are not yet uniform across the EU and even the most elaborate systems remain vulnerable to deception. Furthermore, as far as the trade in conventional weapons is concerned, the development of rigorous national export control systems has, in the major west European arms exporting countries, been offset by commercial opportunity-seeking. This tension was apparent during the Cold War but has come to the fore during the 1990s. The pursuit of commercial opportunity does not sit easily with the development of multilateral – or even national – arms export self-restraint regimes. But if EU governments have so far been wary of a disciplined, centralized export control regime, they have nevertheless made important progress in the 'harmonization' of national definitions, policies and practices. The institutions of the EU – particularly the Commission and the Parliament – have also developed impressive knowledge, if not direct experience, of multilateral arms export regulation. Although a tight, formal regime has not yet come about, and may never, what can at least be said is that the knowledge and practical experience of multilateral arms export regulation in the EU is more advanced than in other, similar initiatives, as is the quality of the debate surrounding these issues.

Much closer cooperation has been achieved in the field of sensitive-technology export control. Pending a full comparison with the successor organization to CoCom, the EU dual-use regulation is unrivalled as a formal, legally based, comprehensive system of technology export control by a group of states. The closeness of this cooperation can be attributed in part to the participation by many EU members in the CoCom exercise. Another contributing factor is the manner in which the European Commission has nurtured common economic, commercial and industrial policies and advanced the cause of the Single European Market. In so doing, the Commission has enabled, or required, governments to cooperate more closely in technology exports. It may also be, finally, that badly regulated technology exports are perceived to be potentially more hazardous in the long term than weapons exports. The reasons for and against weapons exports are relatively easy to discern. Much more demanding is the task of assessing the rationale behind the acquisition of technology and know-how, particularly when the technology in question is dual-use, with both civil and military applications, and especially when militarily useful technology is dual-capable for both conventional weapon and WMD purposes.

To have come this far in the joint regulation of conventional weapon and technology exports is impressive, particularly when set against the more modest achievements of other supply-side export control initiatives. But it is not clear that the EU has yet produced something fundamentally different to, and possibly more durable than, these other initiatives. Will the potential of the EU as an export control regulator be determined by the perceptions of self-interest which drive reactive, contingent, embargo-type initiatives, or will there be agreement upon a set of objective, disinterested values and standards against which exports can be judged? Will there be a convincing rationale for self-restraint? Without such a rationale, and without the discipline of the Cold War or something like it, it is difficult to envisage the international arms trade – and the EU's part in it – being ordered by anything more edifying than national commercial and strategic priorities. Chapters 2 and 3 show that national prerogative is still predominant, even, to a large degree, in the operation of the dual-use regulation. Export control cooperation or 'harmonization' of this nature is more a coincidence of perceptions of national self-interest than a disciplined regime of self-restraint, and the two should not be confused. Agreements can always be made at the lowest common denominator, even in the most difficult policy areas, but they may prove to be more rhetoric than substance. And commitments made in fair weather may be jettisoned when conditions deteriorate. To assess whether the EU has – or could – come up with a new rationale, Chapters 4 and 5 examined European defence industrial consolidation, and European foreign and security cooperation, respectively.

Chapter 4 explored various schemes for restructuring west European defence industry; a necessary task given manufacturing overcapacities and vigorous competition, particularly from the United States. Two points stand out. First, any industrial restructuring or rationalization is likely to involve extra-European exports. The notion that the region's defence industries could be reconfigured in such a way that exports would not be sought or necessary is far-fetched. It is not certain that even the EU defence market would be rich enough to sustain leading-edge defence research, development and manufacturing. What is more, it would require a very courageous – or very foolish – politician to deny a lean, reconstructed and vigorous industrial sector the opportunity to compete in a world market from which other countries were plainly benefiting.

The second key observation is that defence industrial restructuring in the EU is likely to continue to be a slow, incremental and above all inter–governmental (rather than supranational) process. This prediction stems from an analysis of European integration in foreign, security and defence policies made in Chapter 5. Although the EU's Common Foreign and Security Policy will be reviewed in 1996, fundamental change to the consensus-based, intergovernmental structure of CFSP is considered here to be unlikely. The process could certainly be tightened in some areas, but the most that should be expected is 'enhanced intergovernmentalism'.

The lessons to be drawn from these observations – the continued need for exports on the one hand and the preference for cautious intergovernmentalism on the other – are twofold. First, it is important to resist the beguiling, mechanistic logic which moves relatively easily and rapidly from calls for a common European defence equipment market to a need for a common procurement agency, and culminates in a case for a central European export control agency. This logic is attractive, but specious, simply because it assumes that the much slower, more cautious process of political integration can somehow be ignored or outstripped. The same misconception frequently intrudes upon discussion of Article 223 of the EEC Treaty, when arguments for its removal often ignore the reasons for its creation and the case for its retention. The relationship between industrial restructuring and central export control on one hand, and the process of political integration on the other, presents a 'chicken or egg' dilemma of precedence. The sense of this study, however, is that the political will to integrate in areas of 'high politics' will determine the scope and vitality of any institutional arrangements, rather than vice versa. The second lesson to be drawn, implied by the first, is that if cooperation in the management of defence-related trade by the governments and institutions of the EU is to continue, it will in the main take place in less contentious areas and in a non-compulsory, non-binding manner. The political will for an extensive revision of CFSP is uncertain, and as presently constituted neither CFSP itself nor even the joint-action process seem likely to produce centralized policy-making machinery in areas of high politics, including defence-related trade.

This study has also tried to demonstrate that it is not only internal conditions which will determine the EU's effectiveness as a multilateral export control body, but also that there are external factors – practical and conceptual – which limit the potential of the EU. On the practical side, the diffusion of defence manufacturing capability and technological expertise around the world indicates that a significant and growing part of the international trade in these goods is already well beyond the control of the EU. This suggests two things. First, the EU might wish to control its own part in the international arms market, but cannot reasonably expect to be able to regulate the international market as a whole. Second, self-regulation by a limited group of suppliers will encounter the difficulties implied by the argument that 'if we don't export, others will', referred to above and earlier in the study. This argument may not be particularly sophisticated, but its basic political force cannot be overlooked.

Chapter 6 looked at some of the conceptual issues surrounding export controls. For pragmatic, legal and moral reasons, governments are prompted to intervene in defence-related trade. But the perception that 'a unilateral defence sales embargo ... would amount to little more than counter productive gesture politics',[1] persuades these same governments that their national goals might best – or only – be achieved in some multilateral framework. There are two broad types of multilateral regime: hegemonic/denial and cooperative. The political and strategic circumstances of the post-Cold War world push governments towards the second course, and in so doing create a demand for a central organizing principle. There are a number of explanations for this wish to establish a universal code or standard. If, as the diffusion of arms manufacturing capability suggests, control of the international arms trade can no longer be merely a matter of denial, and if the effectiveness of any control regime is proportionate to the number of existing and new weapons exporters participating in it, then there is a requirement to find a new rationale which can both replace military and technological hegemony, and have sufficiently wide appeal. Another explanation could be that when arms exporters have awkward decisions to make, they find it easier to do so in the name of some detached, objective standard for which they cannot be held responsible. Finally, and most simply, international cooperation in any field presupposes some common ground between governments. As the cooperative venture broadens its membership, it becomes more difficult, but also more important, to establish this common ground.

Chapter 6, however, shows the common ground to be meagre. When 'buyer's market' conditions obtain, and when the post-Cold War world is witness to self-confident 'cultural relativism' among recipients and non-

Western suppliers alike, it is too easy for buyers to take the line of least resistance and make purchases of weapons, military equipment and technology unencumbered by the political, moral and cultural baggage of certain suppliers. The rather bleak vision offered by Chapter 6 presents two alternatives in policy terms. First, the notion that multilateral cooperation in defence-related trade should reflect some higher, objective set of values, ethical or otherwise, could be abandoned altogether. There could, arguably, still be scope for principled national decision-making, and for cooperation with like-minded states, but the international arms trade would be understood as a global phenomenon without a global explanation. It might then be, however, that the idea of regulation, either national or multilateral, would prove unsustainable in the face of the 'if we don't export, others will' argument. This in turn would undermine the basic pragmatic, legal and moral considerations which initially persuaded governments that the arms trade should be regulated, and which then drew them into seeking some form of multilateral cooperation. If there is a need for multilateral regulation, there is also a need to find some means by which the initiative can be bound together. Since hegemonic or denial-type approaches are either unfashionable or inappropriate, the discussion returns to the quest for a generally acceptable set of values.

The second, rather less pessimistic position is that objective values can be defined, but only if it is accepted that these values might not be applicable universally. Thus, a group of suppliers might decide to apply conditions regarding human rights, democratic process and government spending to any defence exports, but would do so out of their own conviction. Conditionality of this sort, wherever the source of inspiration, would still be unlikely to appeal to many potential buyers and would present an opportunity for other suppliers. The 'if we don't export, others will' argument would still have force, but then the facts of a buyer's market and feelings of cultural relativism suggest that it always will. What this approach would do is make it easier for a limited number of suppliers, such as the members of the EU, to act in concert and achieve some if not all of the benefits of multilateral cooperation, and may also enable other suppliers and recipients to understand the motives of the collaborating governments and decide on a more informed basis whether or not to cooperate themselves. If standards of behaviour are to be convincing, without being portrayed as universal, they should express the cultural and moral preferences of the political organization from which they spring. What this means is that whatever the political level at which strategic, commercial and foreign policy decisions are made regarding the arms trade, should also be the level from which the values and standards are derived. By this argument, the 'conceptual weakness', referred to at the beginning of Chapter 6, lies not in attempting to apply objective standards to the arms trade, but in applying those standards at an inappropriate political level. For the arms trade to be value-driven requires inquiry not only into the rightness or otherwise of a given export decision, but also into where, when and by whom that decision is made. One widely argued method to achieve a more balanced appraisal of the arms trade involves increasing parliamentary 'oversight' of the decision-making process; it is not that parliamentary involvement would necessarily make any decision more moral, but that open discussion would enable moral arguments to be heard and evaluated, itself an advancement ethically. The least acceptable position, from this perspective, is the one in which the member states and institutions of the EU currently find themselves. At the level of national government, where arms export decisions are made, there is little or no parliamentary oversight, and a tendency to argue that moral considerations can only be admitted once universally acceptable values are identified. Among the institutions, there is similar appeal to universal values, some oversight from the European Parliament, but practically no executive authority. Even in the dual-use regulation, the Commission's authority appears to have been balanced by the retention of sufficient national prerogative. By denying the EU – for whatever reason – the necessary decision-making authority, the unhappy result is that a structurally inadequate political mechanism is tied to universalist ideals, in a formula which fails to convince much of the world. In these circumstances, it is debatable that 'a co-ordinated EC approach would command much greater international credibility than an initiative by a single Member State'.[2]

The EU, its institutions and member governments, and critics of its role as an arms and technology export regulator, are left with two choices. First, it could be argued that national, rather than multilateral, decisions and standards are all that could be expected. For standards to be applied nationally, and to be seen to be applied, would require parliamentary oversight to be increased. This could result in an individual exporter setting an example of good behaviour and helping to limit weapons proliferation through the 'social proof' idea.[3] There would be scope for effective intergovernmental cooperation of the sort achieved in the AG, CoCom and MTCR, although these initiatives depended to a large extent either on the discipline of the Cold War or on the existence of widely held

WMD non-proliferation norms. Governments could seek further 'harmonization' of standards and practices, and in so doing ease some of the difficulties raised by the export of joint-venture weapon systems, develop intelligence-exchange mechanisms, and find ways to involve Europe's defence industries more effectively. Governments could also, finally, promote transparency initiatives such as the UN Register of Conventional Arms – possibly the only international initiative which does not fall foul of the 'Article 51' argument – with the aim of 'exporting' confidence as well as arms. By these means, EU governments might enhance the security of the EU by restricting the spread of key technologies, and would be in a position to deepen their cooperation if and when they decided to give more substance to CFSP. But the drawbacks to this minimalist approach to multilateral defence trade regulation are that the national benefits of multilateral cooperation would be forgone, that it would prove difficult for the expanding EU to accept new partners with possibly sub-standard national export control systems, and that there would still be political and administrative difficulties caused by 'Europeanized' defence industries.

The alternative is to put the EU in such a position that it can devise and project its own standards, and match those standards with an appropriate and effective arms and technology export decision-making process. This view, however, suggests a model of foreign and security policy-making in the EU which is unlikely to develop in the near future. The more likely outcome is that neither option will be selected, and that governments will retain their prerogatives as export controllers while arguing, perhaps disingenuously, that one role of the EU is to define the elusive common ground upon which an effective international code of conduct can be built. In this case, the EU will already have fulfilled its limited potential as a multilateral regulator and will be unable to change the pattern of poor achievement which has so far attended efforts at multilateral regulation of the international arms trade.

The European Union Arms Export Criteria

The Luxembourg criteria, June 1991

- Respect for the international commitments of the member States of the Community, in particular the sanctions decreed by the Security Council of the [UN] and those decreed by the Community, agreements on non-proliferation and other subjects, as well as other international obligations;
- the respect of human rights in the country of final destination;
- the internal situation in the country of final destination, as a function of the existence of tensions or internal armed conflicts;
- the preservation of regional peace, security and stability;
- the national security of the member States and of territories whose external relations are the responsibility of a member State, as well as that of friendly and allied countries;
- the behaviour of the buyer country with regard to the international community, as regards in particular its attitude to terrorism, the nature of its alliances, and respect for international law;
- the existence of a risk that the equipment will be diverted within the buyer country or re-exported under undesirable conditions.

Source: European Council, *Declaration on Non-Proliferation and Arms Exports*, Luxembourg, 29 June 1991.

The Lisbon criterion, June 1992

- The compatibility of the arms exports with the technical and economic capacity of the recipient country, taking into account the desirability that States should achieve their legitimate needs of security and defence with the least diversion for armaments of human and economic resources.

Source: European Council, Lisbon, June 1992.
Note: The original French proposal was to consider the technical and economic capacity of the recipient country, with which Britain, Belgium and Germany were broadly in agreement. Italy, however, wanted to focus on 'legitimate' levels of defence. The final product reflects both approaches.

Notes

Chapter 1: Introduction

1 S. Willett, 'Dragon's fire and tiger's claws: arms trade and production in Far East Asia', *Contemporary Security Policy*, 15/2 (August 1994), p. 114.

2 K. Krause, *Arms and the State: Patterns of Military Production and Trade* (Cambridge: Cambridge University Press, 1992), p. 5.

3 US Arms Control and Disarmament Agency (ACDA), *World Military Expenditures and Armaments Transfers 1993–1994* (Washington, DC, 1995), Table II, p. 91ff.

4 'France overtakes US in arms sales to Third World', *The Times*, 9 August 1995.

Chapter 2: Weapons

1 H. Pelling, *Britain and the Marshall Plan* (London: Macmillan, 1988), p. 4.

2 K. Krause, *Arms and the State: Patterns of Military Production and Trade* (Cambridge: Cambridge University Press, 1992), p. 100.

3 Arms Control and Disarmament Agency (ACDA), *World Military Expenditures and Armaments Transfers (WMEAT)*, 1966–75 (Washington, DC), p. 56.

4 Prohibitions on the postwar Italian defence industry are set out in Articles 51–54, 59, 61 64 and 70 of the Italian Peace Treaty of 10 February 1947; F. Tanner (ed.), *From Versailles to Baghdad: Post-War Armament Control of Defeated States* (New York: United Nations, 1992), pp. 184–7.

5 D. Gerhold, 'Armaments control of Germany: Protocol III of the Modified Brussels Treaty', in Tanner (ed.), *From Versailles to Baghdad*.

6 Stockholm International Peace Research Institute (SIPRI), *The Arms Trade with the Third World* (London: Paul Elek, 1971), p. 216.

7   J. Stanley and M. Pearton, *The International Trade in Arms* (London: Chatto & Windus/IISS, 1972), p. 87.

8   The three-tiered structure is described in Krause, *Arms and the State*, p. 31.

9   R. Harkavy, 'The changing international system and the arms trade', *The Annals of the American Academy of Political and Social Science*, vol. 535 (September 1994), p. 20.

10 ACDA, *WMEAT*, 1965–74, Tables III and IV.

11 ACDA, *WMEAT*, 1971–80, Table II.

12 F. Pearson, 'Problems and prospects of arms transfer limitations among second-tier suppliers: the cases of France, the [UK] and the [FRG]', in T. Ohlson (ed.), *Arms Transfer Limitations and Third World Security* (Oxford: Oxford University Press for SIPRI, 1988), p. 141.

13 ACDA, *WMEAT*, 1991–92, Table III, p. 133.

14 Krause, *Arms and the State*, p. 73.

15 Ibid., p. 73.

16 Ibid., p. 61.

17 H. Mueller, 'The export controls debate in the "new" European Community', *Arms Control Today*, 23/2 (March 1993), pp. 11–12.

18 House of Commons Foreign Affairs Committee, *UK Policy on Weapons Proliferation and Arms Control in the Post-Cold War Era,* vol. II (London: HMSO, March 1995), FCO memorandum dated 6 July 1994, para. 26.

19 'Germany eases rules for weapons exports', *Defense News*, 12 December 1994.

20 See T. Taylor, 'A discussion of techniques for arms transfer controls', in J. Simpson (ed.), *The Control of Arms Transfers* (FCO/BISA Seminar Report, 23 September 1977), pp. 35–6.

21 A.J. Pierre, *The Global Politics of Arms Sales* (Princeton: Princeton University Press, 1982), p. 203.

22 J.M. Lamb and J.L. Moher, *Conventional Arms Transfers: Approaches to Multilateral Control in the 1990s* (Ottawa: CCACD, Aurora Papers no. 13, September 1992), pp. 12–13.

23 See Pearson, 'Problems and prospects', p. 126.

24 Pierre, *Global Politics*, pp. 286, 290.

25 See Tanner, *From Versailles to Baghdad*, p. 212.

26 Assembly of the WEU, Document 500, 4 December 1969; see SIPRI, *Arms Trade*, pp. 108–9.

27 Reply of the WEU Council to the WEU Assembly, 25 March 1970, quoted in SIPRI, *Arms Trade*, p. 109.

28 See Pearson, 'Problems and prospects', p. 147/note 67 for a reference to the Klepsch Report of the EP Political Affairs Committee, 1978.

29 *Report on Arms Procurement within a Common Industrial Policy and Arms Sales*, European Parliament Working Document 1-455/83, 27 June 1983 [Fergusson Report].

30 Fergusson Report, p. 8.
31 European Parliament Working Documents, PE 78.344/fin., 27 June 1983, p. 61.
32 Ibid., p. 62.
33 Pearson, 'Problems and prospects', p. 147.
34 H. Bauer, 'Institutional frameworks for integration of arms production in Western Europe', in M. Brzoska and P. Lock (eds), *Restructuring of Arms Production in Western Europe* (Oxford: Oxford University Press for SIPRI, 1992), p. 38.
35 *Report on European Arms Exports*, European Parliament Session Documents, Series A, Document A2-0398/88, PE 118.374/fin., 22 February 1989 [Ford Report].
36 Ford Report, p. 6, preambular paragraph C.
37 Ford Report, p. 7, preambular paragraphs K and L.
38 Ford Report, p. 23. This had already been recognized by the Committee on External and Economic Affairs (CEEA) in their opinion on the Fergusson Report. The CEEA also noted the argument that a more efficient European defence sector might feel inclined 'to step up rather than reduce overall exports'; CEEA on Fergusson Report, PE 78.344/fin., p. 61.
39 Ford Report, p. 30.
40 Ibid., p. 9.
41 Ibid., p. 8, para. 1.
42 Bauer, 'Institutional frameworks', p. 42.
43 Pearson, 'Problems and prospects', p. 147.
44 Bauer, 'Institutional frameworks', p. 39.
45 *Report on the Outlook for a European Security Policy: The Significance of a European Security Policy and its Implications for European Political Union*, European Parliament Session Documents, A3-0107/91, PE 146.269/fin., 29 April 1991 [Poettering Report].
46 Ibid., p. 8.
47 Ibid., p. 9.
48 Ibid., p. 10.
49 'Resolution on the Community's Role in the Supervision of Arms Exports and the Armaments Industry', European Parliament Resolutions, A3-0260/92, PE 161.873, 17 September 1992.
50 Ibid., p. 64.
51 Ibid., p. 65.
52 'EC nations vote for controls on weapons exports', *The Independent*, 19 September 1992.
53 European Council, *Declaration on Non-Proliferation and Arms Exports*, Luxembourg, 29 June 1991.
54 *Treaty on European Union* [TEU], Title V, Article J.4(1), European Communities No.3 (1992), (London: HMSO, May 1992).

55 TEU Article J.4.1: 'The [CFSP] shall include all questions related to the security of the Union, including the eventual framing of a common defence policy, which might in time lead to a common defence'.

56 See T. Taylor, 'European cooperation on conventional arms exports', ISA Annual Conference, March 1994 (unpublished paper).

57 Saferworld, *Arms and Dual-Use Exports from the EC: A Common Policy for Regulation and Control* (Bristol: Saferworld, 1992).

58 European Parliament Minutes, PE 186.411, Thursday, 19 January 1995 (Provisional Edition).

Chapter 3: Technology

1 G. Hartcup, *The Silent Revolution: Development of Conventional Weapons, 1945–85* (London: Brassey's, 1993), p. xxiii.

2 P. Henderson, *The Unlikely Spy* (London: Bloomsbury, 1993), p. 9.

3 See I. Anthony (ed.), *Arms Export Regulations* (Oxford: Oxford University Press for SIPRI, 1991); Saferworld, *Arms and Dual-Use Exports from the EC* (Bristol, 1992); Export Control Publications, *Worldwide Guide to Export Controls* (Deltac Ltd, 1993 and annually); American Bar Association, *Beyond CoCom – A Comparative Study of Export Controls* (Washington, DC, 1994); and Deltac/Saferworld, *Proliferation and Export Controls: An Analysis of Sensitive Technologies and Countries of Concern* (Deltac, 1995).

4 American Bar Association, *Beyond CoCom*, p. 4.

5 *The Dual-Use and Related Goods (Export Control) Regulations 1995 [DUEC]* (London: HMSO, 1995, SI No. 271), para. 3(2).

6 Export Control Organization, Department of Trade and Industry, *A Guide to Export Controls [Pre-Publication Version]* (London, February 1995), para. 3.3.

7 American Bar Association, *Beyond CoCom*, pp. 22, 109.

8 I. Anthony, 'The United States', in Anthony (ed.), *Arms Export Regulations*, p. 187.

9 M.B. Wallerstein and W.W. Snyder, 'The evolution of U.S. export control policy: 1949–1989', in National Academy of Sciences, *Finding Common Ground: U.S. Export Controls in a Changed Global Environment* (Washington, DC: National Academy Press, 1991), p. 310.

10 'New US licence is key to export ban review', *Jane's Defence Weekly*, 16 April 1994.

11 American Bar Association, *Beyond CoCom*, pp. 11–13.

12 *Federal Register*, 60/91 (11 May 1995), p. 25268.

13 See P. Cornish, *British Military Planning for the Defence of Germany, 1945–50* (London: Macmillan, 1995), Chapter 1.

14 American Bar Association, *Beyond CoCom*, p. 3.

15   C. Hofhansel, 'From containment of communism to Saddam: the evolution of export control regimes', *Arms Control*, 14/3 (December 1993), p. 378.

16   B. Roberts, 'From Non-Proliferation to Anti-Proliferation', *International Security*, 18/1, Summer 1993, p. 165.

17   I. Anthony, 'The co-ordinating committee on multilateral export controls', in Anthony (ed.), *Arms Export Regulations*, p. 209.

18   'The U.S. and multilateral export control regimes', in National Academy of Sciences, *Finding Common Ground*, p. 65.

19   Anthony, 'The Co-ordinating Committee on Multilateral Export Controls', pp. 207–11.

20   T.W. Galdi, 'Advanced weapons technology: export controls before and after the Cold War' (CRS Report for Congress, 93-22 F, 6 January 1993), pp. 7–8.

21   Ibid., p. 8.

22   'Accord near on Cocom successor', *The Financial Times*, 8 November 1993.

23   'Cocom sets stage for successor', *The Financial Times*, 31 March 1994.

24   'Russia can join arms control pact', *Defense News*, 10 July 1995.

25   'Moving towards the New Forum', *BASIC Reports*, No. 46 (20 July 1995).

26   House of Commons Foreign Affairs Committee, *UK Policy on Weapons Proliferation and Arms Control*, vol. II, p. 43.

27   Unnamed British official quoted in 'The successor to CoCom', *BASIC Reports*, No. 43 (15 March 1995).

28   'Dispute delays export control regime', *Defense News*, 14 November 1994.

29   American Bar Association, *Beyond CoCom*, p. 4.

30   For a copy of Order 255/58 of 12 April 1958, the list of products referred to in Article 223(2), see A.C. Allebeck, 'The European Community: from the EC to the European Union', in H. Wulf (ed.), *Arms Industry Limited* (Oxford: Oxford University Press for SIPRI, 1993), pp. 214–16.

31   H. Mueller, 'The export controls debate in the "new" European Community', *Arms Control Today*, 23/2 (March 1993), pp. 10–11.

32   Mueller, 'The export controls debate', pp. 10, 11, and Allebeck, 'The European Community', pp. 193, 194, 207. See also N. Prouvez, 'Implementation and enforcement of an EC arms and dual-use goods export policy', in Saferworld, *Arms and Dual-Use Exports*, p. 88.

33   H. Bauer, 'Institutional frameworks for integration of arms production in Western Europe', in M. Brzoska and P. Lock (eds), *Restructuring of Arms Production in Western Europe* (Oxford: Oxford University Press for SIPRI, 1992), p. 40.

34   *The Financial Times*, 17 February 1992.

35   European Commission, *Export Controls on Dual-Use Goods and Technologies and the Completion of the Internal Market*, SEC (92) 85 (final), 31 January 1992.

36 *Proposal for a Council Regulation (EEC) on the Control of Exports of Certain Dual-Use Goods and Technologies and of Certain Nuclear Products and Technologies*, COM (92) 317 (Final), 31 August 1992.
37 'Council Regulation (EC) No. 3381/94 of 19 December 1994 setting up a Community regime for the control of exports of dual-use goods.'
38 'Council Decision No. 94/942/CFSP of 19 December 1994 on the joint action adopted by the Council on the basis of Article J.3 of the Treaty on European Union concerning the control of exports of dual-use goods.'
39 Council Decision No. 94/942/CFSP, Article 1.
40 American Bar Association, *Beyond CoCom*, p. 99.

Chapter 4: Industry

1 See R. Freeman, 'Opening Statement to HCDC/TISC Inquiry Into Defence Procurement and Industrial Policy', 23 May 1995 (London, Ministry of Defence press release).
2 'One on one' (interview with R. Freeman), *Defense News*, 12 June 1995.
3 'Juppé redefines defense industry in France', *Defense News*, 17 July 1995.
4 W. Walker and P. Gummett, 'Nationalism, internationalism and the European defence market', *Chaillot Papers*, no. 9 (September 1993), p. 45.
5 E. Feuchtmeyer, 'The European armament market – an industrialist's concern', *Military Technology*, 17/10 (1993), p. 45.
6 R. Smith, 'Is Europe pricing itself out of the market?', *Journal of the Royal United Services Institute*, February 1994, p. 48.
7 'A survey of military aerospace', *The Economist*, 3 September 1994, p. 18.
8 K. Krause, *Arms and the State: Patterns of Military Production and Trade* (Cambridge: Cambridge University Press, 1992), p. 58.
9 Feuchtmeyer, 'The European armament market', p. 42.
10 E. Sköns and H. Wulf, 'The internationalization of the arms industry', *The Annals of the American Academy of Political and Social Science*, September 1994, p. 47.
11 'A Eurogun is a tricky thing', *The Economist*, 8 April 1995, p. 84.
12 F. Tusa, 'Aerospace: recovering and fighting', *Armed Forces Journal International*, September 1994, pp. 47–51.
13 'Rebuild allied trade' (leader), *Defense News*, 4 July 1994.
14 For a comment on the incompatibility of the 'Euro-champion' with the Community's 'industrial strategy', see D. Dinan, *Ever Closer Union? An Introduction to the European Community* (London: Macmillan, 1994), p. 368. On the necessity of 'Euro-champions' for the sake of the European defence sector, see Feuchtmeyer, 'The European armament market', p. 45.
15 'Leotard: speed European restructuring', *Defense News*, 19 September 1994; 'Industry plans drift in EU's regulatory limbo', *Defense News*, 29

May 1995; 'Industry urges EU to coordinate defense base', *Defense News*, 3 July 1995.

16 Walker and Gummett, 'Nationalism, internationalism and the European defence market', p. 65.

17 For a pessimistic view of the prospects in the short term, see Smith, 'Is Europe pricing itself out of the market?', p. 50.

18 Sköns and Wulf, 'The internationalization of the arms industry', p. 47.

19 M. Sandström and C. Wilén, *A Changing European Defence Industry: The Trend Towards Internationalisation in the Defence Industry of Western Europe* (Stockholm: Swedish Defence Research Establishment, December 1993), pp. 66, 72. See also Sköns and Wulf, 'The internationalization of the arms industry', p. 56.

20 C. Hofhansel, 'From containment of communism to Saddam: the evolution of export control regimes', *Arms Control*, 14/3 (December 1993), p. 397.

21 T. Enders (DASA), quoted in Sköns and Wulf, 'The internationalization of the arms industry', p. 56.

22 'Industry plans drift in EU's regulatory limbo', *Defense News*, 29 May 1995.

23 See W. Walker and P. Gummett, 'Britain and the European armaments market', *International Affairs*, 65/3 (Summer 1989), pp. 431–2 on SEA Article 30.6(b) and on COM (88) 650 of 17 November 1988, in which the Commission claimed a need to examine defence procurement. Commission forays into this area have often provoked alarm, particularly in Britain; 'EC threat to arms industry', *Sunday Telegraph*, 29 March 1992.

24 Sandström and Wilén, *A Changing European Defence Industry*, p. 73.

25 'BAe instructed not to notify EU', *The Financial Times*, 20 October 1994.

26 Declaration on WEU, C.5.

27 'European defence cooperation', *Military Technology*, 18/6 (1994), pp. 23–33.

28 'British mull position in arms group', *Defense News*, 21 November 1994.

29 'Europe is losing the weapons shoot-out', *Business Week*, 12 June 1995.

30 I. Anthony (ed.), *Arms Export Regulations* (Oxford: Oxford University Press for SIPRI, 1991), p. 2; A.C. Allebeck, 'The European Community: from the EC to the European Union', in H. Wulf (ed.), *Arms Industry Limited* (Oxford: Oxford University Press for SIPRI, 1993), p. 209; Hofhansel, 'From containment of communism to Saddam', p. 395.

31 'Trans-Atlantic harmony faces many obstacles', *Defense News*, 29 May 1995.

32 R.A. Bitzinger, 'The globalization of the arms industry: the next proliferation challenge', *International Security*, 19/2 (Fall 1994), p. 183.

33 S. Willett, 'Dragon's fire and tiger's claws: arms trade and production in Far East Asia', *Contemporary Security Policy*, 15/2 (August 1994), p. 115.

34 I. Anthony, 'The "third tier" countries: production of major weapons', in

Wulf (ed.), *Arms Industry Limited*, p. 380. In *Arms and the State*, p. 141, Krause argues that the urge to export will be especially strong in the second tier.

35 T. Taylor, 'Conventional arms: the drives to export', in T. Taylor and R. Imai (eds), *The Defence Trade: Demand, Supply and Control* (London: RIIA/IIPS, 1994), p. 101.

36 *Defense News*, 13 September 1993.

37 'Offsets: taking a strategic view', *Jane's Defence Weekly*, 5 February 1994.

38 Anthony, *Arms Export Regulations*, p. 86.

39 P. Batchelor and S. Willett, 'To trade or not to trade? The costs and benefits of South Africa's arms trade', *Military Research Group Working Papers*, no. 9 (1995), pp. 5–6.

40 'Pretoria fired up to defy arms embargo', *Sunday Telegraph*, 10 January 1993.

41 B. Roberts, 'From non-proliferation to anti-proliferation', *International Security*, 18/1 (Summer 1993), p. 145.

42 D. Shukman, *The Sorcerer's Challenge: Fears and Hopes for the Weapons of the Next Millennium* (London: Hodder & Stoughton, 1995), p. 193.

43 Ibid., p. 152.

44 See D. Jablonsky, 'The Owl of Minerva flies at twilight: doctrinal change and continuity and the revolution in military affairs', *Professional Readings in Military Strategy*, No. 10 (US Army War College, May 1994).

45 B. Buzan, *An Introduction to Strategic Studies: Military Technology and International Relations* (London: Macmillan/IISS, 1987), p. 27.

46 Willett, 'Dragon's fire and tiger's claws', p. 116.

47 'US Army sees cost savings in dual-use technology', *Defense News*, 21 November 1994; 'Capitol Hill is dual-use battlefield', *Defense News*, 27 March 1995.

48 M. Tapscott, 'Firms putting defense skills to work on smart cars, roads', *Defense Electronics*, February 1994.

49 Freeman, HCDC/TISC statement, 23 May 1995.

50 S.G. Neuman, 'Controlling the arms trade: idealistic dream or realpolitik?', *Washington Quarterly*, 16/3 (Summer 1993), p. 64.

51 M. Moodie, 'Managing technology diffusion and non-proliferation in the post-Cold War era', *International Security Digest*, 2/1 (October 1994).

52 E.J. Laurance, *The International Arms Trade* (New York: Lexington, 1992), p. 167. See also W.H. Reinicke, 'No stopping now: high-tech trade in the new global environment', *Brookings Review*, Spring 1994.

53 P.D. Zimmerman, 'Proliferation: bronze medal technology is enough', *Orbis*, 38/1 (Winter 1994), p. 82. See also D. Mussington, 'Understanding contemporary arms transfers', *Adelphi Papers*, no. 291 (September 1994), p. 20.

54 D.S. Landes, *The Unbound Prometheus: Technological Change and Industrial Development in Western Europe from 1750 to the Present* (Cambridge: Cambridge University Press, 1969), pp. 7, 554.

55 Roberts, 'From non-proliferation to anti-proliferation', p. 148.

56 See M. Kaldor, *The Baroque Arsenal* (London: André Deutsch, 1982).

57 For the British government view, see FCO oral evidence 6 July 1994, in Foreign Affairs Committee Minutes of Evidence, vol. II, p. 43. For the contrasting opinion, see Moodie, 'Managing technology diffusion'.

Chapter 5: Politics

1   M. Smith, 'The Commission and external relations', in G. Edwards and D. Spence (eds), *The European Commission* (Harlow: Longman, 1994), p. 249.

2   B. Soetendorp, 'The evolution of the EC/EU as a single foreign policy actor', in W. Carlsnaes and S. Smith (eds), *European Foreign Policy: The EC and Changing Perspectives in Europe* (London: Sage, 1994), pp. 112–30.

3   Smith, 'The Commission and external relations', p. 251.

4   See S. Nuttall, 'The Commission and foreign policy-making', in Edwards and Spence (eds), *The European Commission*.

5   Ibid., p. 293.

6   *Treaty on European Union* [TEU], Cm 1934 (London: HMSO, 1992).

7   Nuttall, 'The Commission and foreign policy-making', p. 295.

8   M. Holland, *European Common Foreign Policy: From EPC to CFSP Joint Action and South Africa* (London: Macmillan, 1995), p. 12.

9   Smith, 'The Commission and external relations', p. 270.

10 D. Dinan, *Ever Closer Union?: An Introduction to the European Community* (London: Macmillan, 1994), p. 473.

11 Holland, *European Common Foreign Policy*, p. 25.

12 Ibid., p. 227.

13 Ibid., p. 78.

14 Ibid., p. 220.

15 Ibid., p. 225.

16 'Opportunity for fine-tuning', *The Financial Times*, 10 May 1995.

17 'High-level Group of Experts on the CFSP', *European Security Policy Towards 2000: Ways and Means to Establish Genuine Credibility*, Brussels, 19 December 1994.

18 'Pillars of the Community', *Independent*, 4 October 1994.

19 See A. Menon, 'From independence to cooperation: France, NATO and European security', *International Affairs*, 71/1 (January 1995).

20 See 'Britain changes tack to back European power bloc in Nato' and 'Charm offensive: the Foreign Secretary sees the future on French fields' [leader], *The Times*, 28 October 1994. See also P. Cornish, *The Five*

Years' Crisis? European Security after the Cold War, RIIA Briefing
Paper, No. 19 (March 1995).
21 'Rifkind backs WEU as Europe's defence arm', *Guardian*, 31 January
1995.
22 A. van Staden, 'After Maastricht: explaining the movement towards a
common European defence policy', in Carlsnaes and Smith (eds), *European Foreign Policy*, p. 153.
23 Dinan, *Ever Closer Union?*, p. 467 (emphasis added).

Chatper 6: Principles

1 R. Harkavy, *The Arms Trade and International Systems* (Cambridge, MA:
Ballinger, 1975), p. 213; K. Krause, *Arms and the State: Patterns of
Military Production and Trade* (Cambridge: Cambridge University Press,
1992), p. 61.
2 E.J. Laurance, *The International Arms Trade* (New York: Lexington,
1992), p. 4.
3 The legality of supplying arms is discussed in I.D. DeLupis, *The Law of
War* (Cambridge: Cambridge University Press, 1987), p. 66 ff.
4 I. Anthony (ed.), *Arms Export Regulations* (Oxford: Oxford University
Press for SIPRI, 1991), p. 1, and UN Charter Article 2.5.
5 L. Blom-Cooper, *Guns for Antigua* (London: Duckworth, 1990), p. 100.
6 *Treaty on Conventional Armed Forces in Europe and Declarations*
(London: HMSO, March 1991, Cm. 1477).
7 See J. Dean and R.W. Forsberg, 'The future of conventional arms control',
International Security, 17/1 (Summer 1992), and I. Anthony, 'The United
States: arms exports and implications for arms production', in H. Wulf
(ed.), *Arms Industry Limited* (Oxford: Oxford University Press for SIPRI,
1993), p. 77.
8 For a discussion of humanitarian law in respect of anti-personnel mines,
see P. Cornish, *Anti-Personnel Mines: Controlling the Plague of 'Butterflies'* (London: RIIA, 1994).
9 B. Kent, 'A Christian unilateralism from a Christian background', in G.
Goodwin (ed.), *Ethics and Nuclear Deterrence* (London: Croom Helm,
1982), p. 64. See also R. Williamson, *Profit Without Honour? Ethics and
the Arms Trade* (London: CCADD, 1992): 'arms transfers need to be
subordinated to clear moral and political goals'.
10 K. Subrahmanyam, 'Third World arms control in a hegemonistic world',
in T. Ohlson (ed.), *Arms Transfer Limitations and Third World Security*
(Oxford: Oxford University Press for SIPRI, 1988), p. 36.
11 Ohlson, 'Introduction', in *Arms Transfer Limitations*, p. 10.
12 J.G. Stoessinger, *Why Nations Go to War* (New York: St Martin's Press,
1993 [sixth edition]), p. 80.

13 J. Frankel, *International Relations in a Changing World* (Oxford: Oxford University Press, 1988), p. 95.

14 E.J. Laurance, S. T. Wezeman and H. Wulf, *Arms Watch: SIPRI Report on the First Year of the UN Register of Conventional Arms* (Oxford: Oxford University Press for SIPRI, 1993), p. 53.

15 E.J. Laurance, 'Reducing the negative consequences of arms transfers through unilateral arms control', in B. Ramberg (ed.), *Arms Control Without Negotiation* (London: Lynne Rienner, 1993), pp. 176–9.

16 S.D. Krasner, 'Structural causes and regime consequences: regimes as defining variables', in S. D. Krasner (ed.), *International Regimes* (London: Cornell University Press, 1983), p. 1.

17 Ibid., p. 3.

18 P. van Ham, *Managing Non-Proliferation Regimes in the 1990s: Power, Politics and Policies* (London:RIIA/Pinter, 1993), p. 48.

19 O. Young, 'Regime dynamics, the rise and fall of international regimes', in Krasner (ed.), *International Regimes*, p. 98 ff.

20 Group of Seven London Economic Summit, 'Declaration on Conventional Arms Transfers and NBC Non-Proliferation', July 1991, para. 6.

21 For a discussion of an 'incentives-based' approach to arms and dual-use technology transfer regulation, see D. Mussington, *Understanding Contemporary International Arms Transfers* (London, IISS, Adelphi Paper no. 291, September 1994), pp. 48–50.

22 J. Simpson, 'The nuclear non-proliferation regime as a model for conventional armament restraint', in Ohlson (ed.), *Arms Transfer Limitations*, p. 237. See also Laurance, *The International Arms Trade*, p. 55.

23 J.M. Lamb and J.L. Moher, *Conventional Arms Transfers: Approaches to Multilateral Control in the 1990s* (Ottawa: CCACD, Aurora Papers no. 13, September 1992), p. 20.

24 House of Commons, *UK Policy on Weapons Proliferation*, FCO memorandum, para. 24.

25 See S. Ellworthy and P. Ingram (eds), 'International control of the arms trade', *Current Decisions*, no. 8 (April 1992), p. 35, and CCADD, 'The sale and transfer of conventional arms, arms systems and related technology' (London, 1977), p. 9.

26 B. Kellman, 'Bridling the International Trade of Catastrophic Weaponry', *The American University Law Review*, 43/3 (Spring 1994), p. 757 (note 2).

27 Simpson, 'The nuclear non-proliferation regime', p. 231.

28 C.S. Gray, 'Arms control does not control arms', *Orbis*, 37/3 (Summer 1993), p. 333.

29 See A. and H. Toffler, *War and Anti-War: Making Sense of Today's Global Chaos* (London: Warner Books, 1995).

30 Harkavy, *The Arms Trade*, p. 220.

31 J. Keeley, quoted in G. Chafetz, 'The end of the Cold War and the future

of nuclear proliferation: an alternative to the neorealist perspective',
Security Studies (Summer 1993), p. 146.

32   Institute for National Strategic Studies, *Strategic Assessment 1995: U.S.
     Security Challenges in Transition* (Washington, DC, 1995), pp. 187–8.

33   S.P. Huntington, 'The Clash of Civilizations?', *Foreign Affairs*, 72/3
     (Summer 1993). Another exposition of the 'clashing civilizations' thesis
     can be found in A. and H. Toffler, *War and Anti-War*, especially
     pp. 19–28.

34   Huntington, 'Clash of civilizations?', p. 23.

35   Ibid., p. 40.

36   Ibid., p. 47.

37   J. Keegan, *A History of Warfare* (London: Hutchinson, 1993), pp. 387,
     392.

38   H. Bull, *The Anarchical Society: A Study of Order in World Politics*
     (London: Macmillan, 1977).

39   J. Donnelly, *International Human Rights* (Oxford: Westview Press, 1993),
     p. 29.

40   Ibid., p. 30.

41   For these two expressions see, respectively, Donnelly, *International
     Human Rights*, p. 35, and A. Cassese, *Human Rights in a Changing World*
     (Cambridge: Polity Press, 1994 [transl]), p. 50.

42   J. Sachs, *Faith in the Future* (London: Darton, Longman and Todd, 1995),
     p. 66.

43   Quoted in R. Sachi and G. Fikry, 'Dr Mahathir and Malaysia's diplomatic
     agenda', *Asian Defence and Diplomacy*, 1/1 (January 1995), p. 7.

44   Letters, *The Financial Times*, 17 March 1994.

45   'Muslim world to arm Bosnians', *The Times*, 24 July 1995.

46   Letters, *Independent*, 26 January 1994.

47   Letters, *The Economist*, 25 March 1995.

48   'China tells US not to meddle', *The Times*, 3 February 1995.

49   'But the people of China have a stake in the status quo', *The Japan Times*,
     11 January 1995.

50   I. Anthony, *The Arms Trade and Medium Powers: Case Studies of India
     and Pakistan, 1947–90* (London: Harvester Wheatsheaf, 1992), p. 37.
     See also M. Brzoska and F.S. Pearson, *Arms and Warfare: Escalation,
     De-escalation and Negotiation* (Columbia: University of South Carolina
     Press, 1994).

51   *Asian Defence and Diplomacy*, 1/1 (January 1995), p. 28.

Chapter 7: Conclusion

1   C. Masefield, 'Defence exports: the challenge ahead', *Journal of the Royal
    United Services Institute*, 140/4 (August 1995), p. 15.

2 N. Prouvez, 'Arms and dual-use exports in the European Community', in
   J. Dahlitz (ed.), *Avoidance and Settlement of Arms Control Disputes* (New
   York and Geneva: United Nations, 1994), p. 30.
3 G. Chafetz, 'The end of the Cold War and the future of nuclear prolifera-
   tion: an alternative to the neo-realist perspective', *Security Studies*
   (Summer 1993), p. 142.